P9-DBM-587

LOADED

LOADED
Women and Addiction
Jill Talbot

SEAL

Loaded
Women and Addiction

Copyright © 2007 Jill Talbot
Published by Seal Press
A member of the Perseus Books Group
1700 Fourth Street
Berkeley, CA 94710

All rights reserved. No part of this book may be reproduced or
transmitted in any form without written permission from the
publisher, except by reviewers who may quote brief excerpts in
connection with a review.

9 8 7 6 5 4 3

Library of Congress Cataloging-in-Publication Data has been
applied for.

Cover design by Rodrigo Corral Design
Interior design by Stewart A. Williams
Printed in the United States of America
Distributed by Publishers Group West

*Names, places, and identifying details in this book have been
changed or obscured by the author to protect the privacy of
individuals.*

For Indie

Now I'm wine drunk and runnin' with them on my mind
I'm on the backside of thirty and back on my own

—JOHN CONLEE, "Backside of Thirty"

Contents

IV. SIGNIFICANCE

Introduction

When we were kids, Kay and I were best friends. She was tall and skinny, while I was short and stout. A picture of the two of us at age four in a plastic swimming pool testifies to the obvious difference in our stature, though we were convinced we were exactly alike. When we went to Six Flags, both dressed in yellow, with our blond hair in ponytails, we expected strangers to mistake us for twins. When people asked us what we wanted to be when we grew up, I would say teacher. Kay would say go-go dancer. My dad still likes to tell the story of the time Kay came into our kitchen to tell him she was hungry. He told her to eat some Fritos until the burgers were ready. She took one Frito out of the bag and walked out. Sometimes my dad still calls her "One Frito Kay."

Our dads coached football together in a town just outside of Dallas until we were both about six, when her dad got the head coaching job in the small West Texas town of Post. That same year, my dad took the head coaching position at Lubbock High, and both of our moms drove 1976 Monte Carlos, hers in lime green with white leather interior, and mine a maroon one with black leather interior. Since we then lived about forty miles apart, our moms drove those Monte Carlos once a month to Slaton, where we'd eat at a barbeque joint. Kay and I always sat at our own table so we could catch up on whatever lives, whatever secrets we had at that age, convincing ourselves that our conversations were much more interesting and exciting than our mothers'.

Kay and I always had a scheme, some secret that we were convinced we were keeping from our parents. We truly believed that we had a more complex, intricate world than any our parents might know. During that trip to Six Flags, for example, I can only recall the two of us being there, though surely a parent or adult had taken us. I have a picture of the two of us, in our yellow outfits, smiling on the Texas Chute Out, just before the ride stuck and we looked out over the park from two hundred feet. That was how we saw the world, as if we were the only ones who knew what it looked like from that vantage point.

Looking back to those years in West Texas, I remember the pain of stepping on a sticker burr hidden in the thin carpet of Kay's isolated house in Post, the strong winds and tumbleweeds, and the picture I carried of Kay and her cocker spaniel, Champ, in my Velcro wallet for years. Our dads both returned to the Dallas area to coach just as Kay and I were growing out of our matching stuffed animals named Tracy and Stacy and into locker combinations and hushed phone calls from boys. It was a time when our view of the world grew smaller and smaller, like an iris fade in a silent film. We came to know that we weren't alike, that we never really had been. And it went beyond the fact that I'd never eat just one Frito, or that our scheme of pretending to fall asleep in the back seat so that our dads would carry us inside stopped working. What we came to know was that the world had more complicated schemes, and our parents had secrets.

Kay's mom was a smoker, but she didn't want us to know it. But it was hard to miss. After all, she smoked in the back bedroom. It didn't matter that she kept the door closed. I had other friends with parents who convinced themselves that a closed door kept cigarettes a secret. Kay's dad was a smoker and had been for years, but he never hid it. For some reason, around the time we were approaching junior high, her mom started. It bothered Kay, though I'm not sure why. Maybe she didn't like the fact that she was finally old enough to know that her mom might be capable of hiding something from her.

One day Kay stood at that closed door, asking her mom to come out. Kay and I had been nervously waiting for her in Kay's bedroom. Kay had been contemplating how to ask her mom the question she already knew the answer to, and she'd finally worked up the courage to do it. As we sat on the bed, mother stood before the judge, her daughter, and me, the jury, clearly caught by the strong smell of smoke that she wore like a noxious, suffocating perfume. Kay asked, "Are you smoking?" And her mother replied, "Of course not, honey." After her mother left the room, back to another cigarette, I presume, Kay cried. Her mother had lied to her.

I, on the other hand, didn't care that Kay's mom smoked, and even then, I understood her need to hide it. I grew up to be a smoker, just one of my several addictions. Even at a young age, I understood the addict more than the accuser. Somehow, early on, I sensed what it felt like to hide behind that closed door.

When I was a little girl, my mother told me that she worried about me because I had an obsessive-compulsive personality. My mother and I never communicated well, so I didn't ask her what she meant, or why such a personality was cause for concern. But that diagnosis has stuck with me all these years, one of the most hurtful things I've known, and at times I wonder if I didn't end up living a mother-imposed prophesy. For as I grew older, I began to notice my propensity for taking everything too far, or at least as far as I could. By the time I was thirteen, I had had my first beer; by the time I was fifteen, I was a weekend drinker, though I was known as the girl at the party to watch out for, because I'd be out of control with boys or booze or both.

By the time I was thirty-five, I was sitting in a group circle at rehab, learning that most alcoholics start drinking by age thirteen. I spent the summer of my sixteenth year grounded for getting drunk at a party, but for all my parents' discipline, warnings, and restrictions, I couldn't quell my craving for trouble, whether that was taking the car out without permission or giving Billy Tucker, the school druggie, twenty bucks for a bag of hearts (Dexedrine). I weighed one hundred and fifteen pounds at the time, and the hearts were another trick I tried, along with laxatives and vomiting. Whatever I did, I did do it obsessively, and it was more often than not something I had to hide.

Trouble, as I grew older, shifted from high school weekend parties at Tammy Anderson's house to dance clubs in college, where I'd accept any drug offered to me, whether it was Ecstasy from the guy I went with or some stuff I sniffed from a brown vial offered to me by the transvestite who danced up to me during "White Lines." I stopped doing things like that only after I woke up in the back seat of a car with a group of strangers screaming at me. Only when I realized I could die and no one would know where I was did I pull back a bit on my behavior and stay home the next weekend. Then, a few weeks later, I did whip-its while driving and wrecked my car. At some point, my predilection for taking risks turned to men, and I slept primarily with married men, a trip that lasted throughout my twenties. In my thirties, I settled down with one man, "My Blue-Collar Man," I called him, and we lived together and had a daughter. That little girl, Indie, is five now, and that blue-collar man is long gone.

When Kay and I were five, we'd get on the phone for what seemed like hours and revise the nursery rhyme "Georgie Porgie." We took turns adding to the first line, which we altered to, "Georgie Porgie had no panties." I'd say, "Georgie Porgie had no panties/He went to the store and he had no panties." And Kay, after recovering from a full-body giggle, would offer, "Georgie Porgie had no panties/He had a dog but he had no panties." I still laugh when I think of us, entertained by exhibitionist Georgie and his adventures. The other day, I was reading to Indie and came across the real

"Georgie Porgie." There's no mention of scantily clad young men, only a young man kissing girls, making them cry, and running away. I know the rhyme better than I thought. And I also know that that iris fade of my youth has expanded into a view of the world I could never have imagined. Nothing in my life is what I expected it to be, a fact I can now attribute to my addictions, my compulsions, and my obsessions.

When I began this book, I wanted to tell the story of how My Blue-Collar Man left me, but as I began going back into the patterns and the people that led me to him, a background emerged: alcohol. So many of my stories, including the ones about myself, are about women who have an addiction of one kind or another. Whether it was their addiction or my own—to alcohol, cigarettes, secrets, men, or heartache—all of our lives were characterized by a severe theme of hiding. My mother and my father hid a great deal from me, and they still do, which is how I know how debilitating and damaging the secrets of a family, or even a lifestyle, can be. I also know how distracting men can be, how I can lose myself in them, and how many of my friends have done the same.

My own addictions have affected many people, emboldening or sometimes burdening our relationships. This book is my way of giving a voice not only to my addictions, but also to women like Kay's mom, who have at one time or another felt that addiction is something they deal with alone, behind a closed door—women who have had a habit, a passion, a memory, a man, or an addiction they couldn't shake and couldn't share. One of the most intense addictions I have witnessed in my life is my mother's to her privacy, to the secrets she holds close, so if you ever happen to run into her, please pretend, the way she does, that none of this ever happened.

Secrets

1. My Grandmother's Flowers

We hide our secrets within our art. My grandmother painted flowers. Roses, mostly, and daisies against dark backgrounds of muted golds and smudged grays, which made for an unsettling scattering of stems and petals attached to nothing. She also lined the bookshelves of her living room with her small painted pitchers, their delicate handles outlined in gold. On the walls of her rooms were ghosts from the years when she could steady a brush against a canvas or a ceramic pitcher. The largest painting, of what must have been at least two dozen, hung over the uncomfortable couch in her living room. The roses were rich, soft red, their stems long, thorny. About thirty roses, looking as if they had been dropped on the ground, as if someone had walked away from them in surrender. An ornate gold frame emblazoned their melancholic majesty. It was my mother's favorite.

My mother painted too, mostly in black and white, as if her secrets were stripped of all color. One of her paintings is of an outhouse, black acrylic scratched onto a white canvas. When she was growing up, she had a recurring dream that she had walked out into the night (she was indeed a sleepwalker as a child) and found herself chopped up into small pieces in the outhouse. To this day, she will not leave a knife lying in the sink or on a kitchen counter at night. Somehow,

her subconscious even snuck into my own phobias. I follow the same ritual, checking the kitchen for knives before
bed, as if the horror of her childhood might find me. And it
often has, as the rhythms of our parents, our grandparents,
beat beneath our own surface. Other patterns skip, I've noticed, pick up in another generation. I do not paint, though I
tried when I was younger. I could not wrap my mind around
how to reveal the image in my imagination on a canvas. I
couldn't even begin a line, or start the curve of a brush. I
became a writer instead, using words to paint pictures, to
unravel the knots that were tied long ago.

I did not know my grandmother very well; either she
kept to herself or my mother kept her from me. We'd visit her at Thanksgiving and Christmas, and sometimes my
mother and I would drive the hour and a half on a weekend afternoon in the summer. But more often than not, a
planned trip to my grandmother's house in Mt. Pleasant
would be canceled at the last minute. I'd hear the phone
ring in the kitchen before the sun came up, my mother's
hushed voice echoing down the hall. At breakfast she'd an-
nounce, "We're not going," and my father and I would trade
glances, knowing not to say anything more about it. Sometimes we'd make it as far as the gas station in Mt. Pleasant, and my mother would make a call from the pay phone
outside and then get back in the car and say, "Turn around."
There were even occasions when we made it all the way to
the back porch, where my mother would sigh heavily and
then quietly knock on the screen door, as if she were afraid
of waking a stranger.

Silence weighed down my grandmother's house. And cigarette smoke. Nights in her house were creepy. I'm not sure there's a better word for it. After we'd all go to bed, the light in my grandmother's room would stay on, the clink of a glass ringing out as loud as the chimes from the grandfather clock in the living room. One of those nights, I woke up to my mother's face in the darkness of the room. She swept me out of the house, and we scurried away to a motel on Interstate 30, she still in her nightgown, with something heavy, which I was too young to recognize as shame, hanging on her like a long coat.

I was eleven years old when my mother finally told me that my grandmother was an alcoholic. It was a Saturday afternoon in early fall, and my mother and I were visiting my grandmother for the weekend. I was washing my hair in the kitchen sink, something I often did at home, sometimes more than once a day. Just as I had put the conditioner through my hair, my mother leaned over me and whispered firmly that we had to leave the house immediately. I started to say something about the conditioner, but after so many years of sudden departures and hushed exchanges, I obeyed without hesitation and wrapped a towel around my head as I headed out the back door toward the car. I sat in the car for over an hour, nervous and a little scared. The conditioner in my hair dried in the meantime, making it thick and greasy.

On the way home, my mother sobbed into the steering wheel and asked me if I knew what it meant to be an alcoholic. I quietly said yes, though I wasn't quite sure. I imagined it had something to do with lights under bedroom doors at night, early morning phone calls, and Budweiser cans instead of green beans lining the cabinets. My mother stopped at a steakhouse on the way home; looking back, it seems odd to have stopped in public after such an emotional release. I assumed she wanted to talk with me face to face. But nothing. During our lunch at K-BOB'S, where I sat across from her, feeling self-conscious about my matted hair, she didn't mention any of what had transpired.

After that trip, I saw my grandmother just once a year until I left home, when I decided to try to have a relationship with her on my own terms. I felt as if I were not allowed to get to know her, to find out if there was anything redeeming about her. In my mother's eyes, she was an alcoholic, nothing more.

Around that time, as I entered adolescence, my mother and I fought. We'd scream at each other, and I'd cry until I was exhausted. When I think of us during those difficult years, I remember the gold carpet in our dining room, the chandelier forcing too much light into the room, the large mirror I still cannot look into when I pass it for fear that I'll be taken back to the day when I screamed at her, "You're a bad mother!" She slumped to the floor, crying into the carpet, and I stood above her, stunned by the emotion she so rarely allowed herself.

"Does your mother get so drunk that she thinks the carpet is flowers?" she asked, looking up at me, as if begging. I felt guilty. I knew nothing of her childhood; in fact, I had never even considered the idea that she had once been a child. Like most teenagers, I embodied a skewed sense of propriety. "Does she grab your leg as you try to run out of the room and ask you to smell the pretty flowers, holding one up to you?" In that moment, she transformed before my eyes. I saw my grandmother in her, running her fingers along the carpet until she found a flower and picked it, holding it up to me with a face of confused wonderment. I felt afraid. I had broken into the graves of my mother's memory, exhuming the frightened child and the stranger her mother had been to her all those years. In the years that followed, I learned that a mother does not have to be drunk to hurt her daughter with words.

We wouldn't speak of her childhood again until after my grandmother's death in 1997. My mother has since told me that she used to find her mother naked and passed out in the hallway when we'd show up for visits, how she used to walk home from school and find the living room, the kitchen, littered with empty bottles and vomit, her mother passed out in the bedroom. But even now, most of her childhood remains a secret to me. I realize how the family pattern has continued, how I do not know my mother very well at all. There are snippets: I know she had a boyfriend in college named Danny, that she liked to wear hats in the 1960s, that she likes to take baths. I also know that she learned how to love from her mother, and because of that there has always been and always will be a distance between us.

My grandmother was a hairdresser in the 1940s, engaged to a man named Robert Johnson. Robert was called overseas to fight in the war, like so many young men of his generation. While he was away, a man named Joyce Stinson, known by everyone in the county as "Chubby," asked my grandmother to dance one summer night at a gathering in the neighboring town. He was a large man with small facial features, squinty eyed and big boned. "I can't dance with you," she told him. She didn't want to dance with anyone but Robert. But Chubby was persistent. He got her to go outside to take a look at his new truck. He offered her some moonshine, which she refused, and then called her the next day at her beauty shop. Initially, she refused to go out with him, but he must have been persuasive—perhaps even charming—enough to change her mind.

My grandmother ended up writing Robert a "Dear John" letter and marrying Chubby Stinson. They moved to a white house outside Mt. Pleasant, and Chubby set up a makeshift gambling room in a small shack at the back of their property. She'd often go there to reclaim him, the only woman in a room full of drunken men and smoke, shuffling cards and pouring sweat. The first few times she tried quietly to persuade him to come home; eventually, those polite requests transformed into loud interruptions and demands. But nothing changed. "Go on home, Lucille," he'd snarl at her. They had one child, and my grandmother nearly died in the delivery. She resented her daughter, her loneliness, herself. She started drinking. She never stopped.

When I left home, I decided I was old enough to make my own decisions about whom I would love. I began writing my grandmother letters, and she would return them when she could, when she was sober enough to write. Many of her responses were spread out across several days, sometimes weeks. Monday would be written like a heading, followed by a few paragraphs that dissolved into a shaky scrawl, until she resumed on Thursday. During the last few years of her life, she wrote almost weekly, and I visited whenever I went back home. Some of those visits were clandestine. I hid them from my mother out of respect for the distance she enforced. I realized that I had never been alone with my grandmother, and I assumed that my mother's choices stemmed from her fear that I would see my grandmother drink, or worse; but as I got to know my grandmother better, I suspected that my mother's real fear might be for what my grandmother might reveal.

Yet my grandmother's words only exposed a kindness toward my mother that I never witnessed when the two were together. I even heard a story of her surprise visit to my mother when she was in college. My mother's best friend and roommate answered the door, and while my grandmother waited in the bedroom, she noticed two cigarettes burning in an ashtray on the windowsill. She smiled in her recollection, and I wondered if the smile was more about having caught her daughter smoking than about the story itself. But she never said anything about it to my mother. In one way, I suppose she couldn't, given her own smoking, but it seemed to me to be an allowance my own mother never emulated.

My grandmother grew more eccentric as the years passed, with an apparent progression in her idiosyncrasies. She started buying dozens of one thing, like small jewelry boxes or can openers, demanding every time I visited that

I go back into her bedroom to choose something from her latest collection. One year when I called on her she spent the entire visit walking through her house behind a grocery cart. The cart was filled with random items—toilet paper, a curling iron, an outdated issue of *McCall's*. She was a bag lady in her own home. She always had two cigarettes going, one in the ashtray, another dangling from her lips. And she had the greatest ashtrays, either the standing kind or the ones with twenty indentations around the edges, made during the days when everyone at the table needed a groove for her cigarette.

Strangely, I never saw her drink. And I wanted to. I wanted to see firsthand what had been hidden from me all my life. Besides that, I wanted my grandmother to feel that she could be herself around me, or that we could obliterate all of my mother's taboos and have a drink together. There was no alcoholic I could recognize, just a lonely woman who smoked and threw her money away on junk and lottery tickets. Before opening her back screen door, I'd brace myself for any version of my grandmother I might find, but each time I'd find only what anyone would expect a grandmother to be, a woman who asked about my school and my boyfriend, my friends and my future. To be honest, I felt let down, as if I had steeled myself for a monster and instead found a nice lady whose laughter brought on fits of coughing. She was more pathetic than anything, a monument to years of self-destruction.

I did finally get to see her drink during my last visit to her house, the last time I saw her, as she and I sat at the kitchen table, a big plastic tumbler of vodka and a full ashtray of cigarette stubs before her. She took a long drag, coughed, and told me she was making me the executor of her estate. I knew she was doing it out of spite, a final malicious act against her daughter, as if all the glasses emptied over the years had not produced a deep enough wound. From that moment until she died, I dreaded the idea of her passing. I didn't see her a single time during that final year of her life, because I was attending graduate school in another state and rarely went back to Texas. I heard that she became increasingly dependent upon neighbors, the kindness of those strangers who took her signed checks to buy groceries or pay the electric bill, and that in return she put their children through school, paid off their mortgages, or built them a house on Lake Bob Sandlin.

Her house had yellowed walls, drawers of photographs, and a brown sack of unopened Jim Beam in a shoebox. The price tag reflected the fact that it was not a recent purchase. She had hidden liquor even from herself. The day I packed up the life of a woman who had always been elusive, I smoked cigarettes and stubbed them out in all the ashtrays, the standing one next to her chair, the cattle one on the kitchen counter, the rose glass one by her bed. As I packed away pillowcases and church keys, I drank a six-pack of Budweiser I'd bought at the gas station we used to stop at on the way into town, where my mother used to call from the pay phone while I waited in the back seat.

For me it was a ceremony, an offering to a woman who had ultimately allowed her addictions to take over her life.

I considered the six-pack and cigarettes an appropriate way to honor the passing of my grandmother as I emptied her home. The carpets were gouged with holes from when her bony fingers couldn't steady even a cigarette, and the upholstery of the couches and the armchairs was all punctuated with perfect black circles.

My mother had refused to help me with the estate handling, though she did ask me to make sure I thumbed through every magazine, every bible, every book on the off chance that my grandparents had left behind some of the cash reserves they used to stash between such pages. The only thing I found was a list of songs my grandmother wished to have sung at her funeral and a stack of old lottery tickets. I also found a photograph of my mother as a little girl. The black ringlets of her hair, the overalls. She was climbing a fence, the shadow of a figure—my grandmother, taking the picture—across her. She had one leg raised in escape, and I then knew the truth: She never got away.

Beyond the silence and the cigarettes of my grandmother's house, there were the secrets. And that afternoon, I discovered another one. There were no paintings on my grandmother's walls, just white squares standing out in the yellow of smoke-stained walls. Later there was some speculation that she had promised them to one of her caregivers, a nurse who had stayed with her during the last year of her life. My grandmother was always making impetuous promises, offering accolades to those she barely knew and never extending good words to her daughter. It thus seemed befitting that she might have ultimately granted the most intimate and beautiful thing about herself to a near stranger.

The paintings' absence was eerie. No signatures, no gold frames, and only three of the painted pitchers sat on top of the encased bookshelf. At one time, there had been twenty-seven. It was clear that someone had gotten into the house, invited or not, though it felt as if the entrance had been clandestine and guilty, the paintings stolen. When my mother told me, "Someone got into the house and took every painting and the jewelry she kept in her safe," I couldn't help but suspect her. After all, she had every right to take them, to take everything. Maybe she feared I would not relinquish them to her. About a year ago, my grandmother's lawyer wrote to inform me that a "friend" had returned the jewelry, admitting that it was rightfully mine. When I called to tell my mother, suggesting that she pick up the jewelry, she got quiet. If she was indeed the "friend," I wondered, how did she feel about my returning the gesture?

My mother claims she cried for the loss of the red roses. And before I took the trip to pack up the house, she asked me to look carefully, saying that her mother could have stashed the paintings and the rest of the pitchers under her bed, in a closet, in the garage. I found only one painting, of a round, transparent green vase full of daisies, the background a dull green brushed with yellow. Two daisies out of the vase, with crossed stems. It was one of the brightest paintings she had done. There was always a feeling of something separate, something being discarded, in my grandmother's paintings. I think it must have been how she saw herself.

I tell my own daughter how beautiful and good she is

every day. I tell her other things, too—about my day, the movie I saw the night before, the book I'm reading, the song I used to sing for neighbors when I was only six. I want her to know me. I want to know her. More than anything, I want her to know herself, and to not be ashamed or afraid or alone. I also want her to know where she comes from, and so her great-grandmother's painting, the one of the daisies, hangs in her room.

I still have a mental image of my mother on the day of my grandmother's funeral, standing in the center aisle before the service. She wore red, a shock of color, all scorn and guilt. A gray casket in the front of the chapel, my grandmother in a pink gown, all the flowers she had once painted arranged around her in a delicate and heavy frame. My father later told me that my mother had held on to his arm and said, "I am a stranger here." Meanwhile, I had been in the other room, telling the preacher how my grandmother and I had written letters, how she had shared with me the story of meeting my grandfather, how she always had a pumpkin pie for me at Thanksgiving. I suppose I was trying to prove something by letting the preacher, a stranger himself, know that someone had cared about this woman, that someone had known her, had loved her. Looking back, I don't think any one of us—my mother, my grandmother, or I—knew the others, or if any of us gave each other the chance to, all of us fighting to undo each other's guilt while absolving our own. We loved as little as we knew how to. It was too much in the end, I think—all of us mothers, daughters, strangers.

2. A Part of Me

My father listens to Jerry Lee Lewis records every morning as he gets ready for work and every afternoon when he comes home.

> Mornings come and Lord my mind is achin', yes it is
> Sunshine standing quietly at my door
> Just like the dawn my heart is silently breaking
> With my tears it goes tumbling to the floor. . . .

He used to be a big drinker, until my mom threatened to leave him if he didn't stop going to the bar every night. I think he must have brought songs back from that smoky bar, because even though he never drank again, he raised me with drunk and lonesome men like Merle Haggard, Jerry Lee Lewis, Waylon Jennings, and Kris Kristofferson. I think he lives the life he misses through songs. And even though I'm a professor and a city girl, all the years of listening with him put regret and honky-tonks in me, too, because I knew of ramblin' men who rode whiskey rivers at too early an age. I feel just as comfortable in some hole-in-the-wall bar as I do in a classroom. I used to think that I must have been a barfly in a past life, until I figured out that I actually was one, at age six, in my own living room. My dad would call me over to his record player and put his earphones on my head. Those earphones never fit, but the words I was listening to did; even then, I understood what those bearded men were singing and why.

My dad's record player is a large, cherry wood console he bought in 1970, the year I was born. In the evenings after he got home from football practice, or on weekend afternoons after he had mowed the lawn, he would lie down on the floor with a pillow behind his head, propping himself up against the console to listen through his big black-and-beige earphones, the earpieces taking up the entire sides of his head. I once asked him why he listened that way, instead of through the speakers, and he said he could hear the words and the background music better; plus, it knocked out the noise. I wondered at first if that noise he was talking about was me, or maybe a noise within him he wanted to block out. Or maybe it was as simple as my mother's request to not have to listen to Waylon Jennings one more time.

My father has a habit of listening to the same song again and again, and I've inherited this trait. For the past two years, it's been Jerry Lee Lewis, a man who sings about the women who left him, the mistakes he knows he's made, the paychecks he spends on Fridays at the bar. Jerry Lee now appears in concert twice daily through the speakers of the thirty-five-year-old console, the one with the small green light at the bottom that shines when it's on. My dad plays the records loud enough that he can hear them while he's in the shower; if you're in the house during concert hours, it's as if Jerry Lee himself is in the back room, remembering a woman he'd rather forget after having a few, though that's what made her go in the first place.

Dad has several of Jerry Lee's records, ones he bought as they were released through the years, and ones I buy for him at music stores that still carry vinyl. But he tends to play one more than the others: *Another Place Another Time*, side A, song one: "She Even Woke Me Up to Say Goodbye."

Of course, like many of Jerry Lee's ballads, the words of that song are even more haunting and sad in Jerry's voice, in the heavy chords he plays on the piano. But they're not nearly as sad unless you know why my father listens to them at least once a day, sometimes twice in a row. He'll be seventy-two this August, and he's still in his room with Jerry, singing words to his own memory of the woman who went away.

> Once again, the whole town will be talking, yes they will
> And Lord I've seen the pity that's in their eyes. . . .

My father, a preacher's son, was an athlete, an impressive one. During the late 1940s, he wore #10 for the North Dallas Bulldogs. Each time he made a touchdown, one of the more prominent men in town would give him $2. During one game, he made fourteen bucks. He earned a scholarship to Stephen F. Austin University to play football and baseball. It was the early 1950s, and most college boys, my dad among them, got to and from school by hitchhiking. After one of his baseball games, some men asked my dad and some of his teammates to go to Louisiana and play professionally for the summer. A few of my dad's buddies leapt at the chance and took off, but my dad said he didn't feel right about it because it would ruin his eligibility. Even after the men assured him that no one would find out, he still declined. I sometimes wonder what his life might have been like, as I'm sure he does, if he had gone to Louisiana to play ball instead of getting married at twenty and having a son he named Rodney, after one of his best friends.

> They could never understand it's her sorrow, it's not a man,
> No matter what they say, we know she tried. . . .

I know very little about my father's first wife beyond her addictions and her disappearance. About a year ago, I was visiting my dad during the summer. He took me to a Texas Rangers baseball game, as he does every time I visit during the season. On the hour-and-twenty-minute drive back home, he started talking about Geraldine, Gerry. He had never talked about her, so I held still, afraid that one small movement on my part would interrupt the trance he seemed to be in. It was as if the darkness, the night at the ballpark, his eyes on the road, afforded him a space in which to remember. I already had pieces of the story from my half-brother Rodney, sixteen years older than I, but what I didn't get until that night was my father's lack of understanding, his unanswered questions, his regret, his guilt.

She was a tiny woman, about four foot ten, a drinker and addicted to pills. She once kicked a hole in the windshield of my dad's car because she didn't want to go to Thanksgiving dinner at his parents' house. She once took two pans full of boiling water into the bedroom where her husband and her five-year-old son were sleeping and threw it on them because she was mad at something my father had said hours earlier. He eventually put her in an institution; he described the afternoon he left her there—the way he went to his empty car feeling as if he had betrayed her.

The doctors called him within a week, though, and asked him to come pick her up. They said they could not control her, that they couldn't do anything in the face of her paranoid schizophrenia. His voice held the confusion and hopelessness he must have felt back then. He seemed to feel compelled to convince me she had once been a different woman. "She was good and loving to me and ol' Rod," he told me. Gerry was back for only a few months before she disappeared. It took the police over a month to find her, though they didn't really find her—just evidence of her mania, my father's car on the side of the road at least six hundred miles away, liquor bottles and cigarettes, dirty clothes, puddles of rain on the floorboards. My father never saw her again.

> Baby's packed her soft things and she's left me,
> She's left me, she's left me.
> And I know she didn't mean to make me cry. . . .

She didn't even show up to the courthouse for the custody hearing. My father had to prove nothing that day; her absence was enough to grant him full custody, and so for years it was just the two of them, a man and his son. My brother has told me stories of those years, suggesting that our father worked hard to drink and fuck his way out of the misery of a failed marriage and a missing woman. During their marriage, Gerry hid piles of bills in the drawers. She even had Rodney do it for her, and promise not to tell; and he loved her, so he kept her secret, even though he had no idea what he was doing, what he was keeping secret. By the time my father found out about their debt, he was facing a policeman at his apartment door and the truth that his wife had spent well beyond their means. The Talbot men were broke, and for a time they lived in a car, until my dad finally took his son to live with his parents. I suppose he could no longer face Rodney, knowing he had nothing to offer him beyond his own weariness and guilt.

My father stopped talking at some point in his reminiscing to ask if I minded his talking about this, about her. I could tell it didn't really matter what I said—he needed to tell me. I think he wanted me to know that his memory had blanks, unanswered questions. The father of my child had just left me, and I never saw it coming. I think my father wanted me to know that he felt compassion, that the unanswered questions were part of how these things went. Maybe my dad was trying to tell me his own story so that I might know my own. People leave us and we don't know why. Sometimes we do everything we can, and they still want out. Not from us, but from themselves, and sometimes we're too close to them to allow for such escapes.

> It's not her heart Lord it's her mind,
> She didn't mean to be unkind.
> Why, she even woke me up to say goodbye. . . .

When I visit my parents and hear Jerry Lee in the afternoons, or am awakened by the chorus of "She Even

Woke Me Up to Say Goodbye" at 6:30 AM, I hurt for the man who never even got that. Gerry died in 1996, in her driveway, from an aneurism. My brother went to her funeral, shaken by the sight of her second family, by a brother he didn't know beyond an afternoon visit from a stranger at his door. She had followed what he had been doing to a certain extent. Someone in our family had sent her notices and updates: newspaper clippings of his football career, his wedding announcement, his business, address, phone numbers. She wrote occasional letters and made random phone calls that served as reminders that she was aware of where he was, what he was doing, his wife's name, the names and ages of his children. Small reminders that somewhere he had a mother. Not long before she died, he took a trip to Phoenix to see her. He said she remained a pathological liar, a woman who looked him in the eye and made up stories. He said she had not changed.

Gerry is a mystery my father keeps locked up deep inside, but sometimes, if I ask at just the right time, I'll get another insight into this piece of him that I want to better understand. My parents' song is "Yesteryou, Yesterme, Yesterday," by Stevie Wonder, a song that begins: "What happened to the world we knew?" I once asked my dad why they had chosen that song; it's not exactly a love song, but more of a loss song. His quick answer was that it was popular when they were dating. After another minute or two, though, he admitted that he and my mother came to each other with dreams that hadn't worked out, lives they had to let go, a feeling that what they had really wanted in life was not going to work out. I suppose two people who come to each other so broken have nothing to do but mend and start something anew, even if it means facing the reality that things aren't going to turn out the way they'd once imagined. Apparently, it has been enough to sustain them for more than thirty-five years.

Last year my father and I found out that he isn't the only one with a connection to Jerry Lee Lewis. My mother was sitting in the back seat while we were headed to some Mexican restaurant in Dallas, telling us how she had worked at a radio station in high school. One afternoon, she said, Jerry Lee Lewis came in with his new record. It was 1962. He asked her to be the president of his fan club in the small East Texas town of Mt. Pleasant. I turned around in shock, while my father kept his eyes on the road and shook his head. Why, after all these years, had she not mentioned this? In all of our discussions of Jerry Lee, what had kept her from telling us she had the closest connection of all? Sure, my mother is a private person, and she offers information in her own time, but thirty-five years and countless hours of Jerry Lee records playing exaggerated her secret to an almost grotesque degree. All this time, my father had had a singer who gave a voice to his sadness, and the whole time my mom was the president of his fan club. That seemed about right to me.

There is a large part of the story that my father left out that night. It's about me, in a way, about a part of me. I only know it because my brother told me. My middle name is Lynn, after my half-sister. When Rodney was five, his mother had another baby, a girl. She lived for thirty minutes. Rodney says he still can remember Dad holding him up to the window of the hospital to see his mother inside. He was not allowed in the hospital, though he says that even that day, he felt she was already gone. Doctors say that the death of her baby triggered Gerry's mental illness. Now that I have a little girl of my own, I know that such madness is surely justified. I too would have locked myself away. As I write this I am remembering a woman, an afternoon, in a hospital in Nacogdoches, Texas, that I never knew, but I can see my father crying in the hallway of the hospital. I have only seen him cry twice, but it destroys me, the way parents' tears do; if we have good parents, we feel that if they fall apart, there will be nothing left of us. I am sure that what my father has carried in silence all these years has destroyed him in more ways than one.

Rodney says that Lynn's grave is in a cemetery in a North Texas town that no longer exists, and when he passes through the area he stops, though he says he's never been able to find the marker. I cannot imagine a life shadowed by such mystery, a mother who drove away, a sister who did not live, but my brother does not listen to Jerry Lee Lewis. He likes the Stones and Elvis, prefers to pretend that Jerry Lee Lewis isn't singing for him, too. "She Even Woke Me Up to Say Goodbye" was released the year I was born, so even though I did not live this story, it is somehow mine.

> She didn't mean to be unkind.
> Why, she even woke me up to say goodbye,
> Goodbye baby. . .

3. What Little I Know Is Enough

When I was growing up, my mother kept one of her pen and ink drawings in the bathroom. A small work of an outhouse, black acrylic scratched onto a white canvas. I was too young to get the irony, too naive about art to ask her why she drew it. I haven't seen that outhouse for years, which makes me wonder if she even kept it, or if she took it down for something as simple as a change of decor. Even if I asked her, I'm not sure she'd give me the answer I want. She rarely does, but even so, I've found answers without her even knowing I've asked the questions, and clues without ever having searched.

Not too long ago, when I was visiting my paternal grandmother, she told me about an afternoon when my mother came to her, sobbing and hugging her, crying the words: "I've never felt loved." I felt sorry for my mother, as I often do, but I respected her privacy, too, and chose not to ask my grandmother for more. Also, I didn't know what to say, distracted by questions: *What about me? What about my father?* Maybe she meant maternal love. After all, she often tells me that her mother-in-law's house is the only place she can truly relax. I also remembered my father telling me how my grandmother had told him, "She's cold," when she'd first met my mother nearly forty years earlier. So it was good to know my mother had finally found a place, a home, in which she could voice her feelings of being unloved, but on my drive home I felt troubled, wondering how my father and I may have failed her, too.

I thought about my mother, with her alcoholic mother and distant, gruff father, her isolated childhood—in a white house in the country in the late '40s and early '50s. She was a sleepwalker living near a highway, and her father once found her just a step away from that road before turning her around and leading her back to the house. She told me that story when I was little, when I started sleepwalking myself. As I got older, and understood better what her childhood was really like, I wondered if she had been escaping in her sleep, opening a screen door in the dark in hopes that daylight would not bring her back home.

The recurring dream my mother had as a child was never intended for me to know. I read it one afternoon in the dining room among a stack of her papers, apparently an answer to some assignment. There, unable to pull myself away, I gained uninvited access to my mother's thoughts and fears—that dream and her fear of knives, why she'll cringe at any blade not tucked away in the drawer or the dishwasher. I've learned more about my mother from other people or overheard conversations, or by connecting pieces, than I've ever learned from her. The outhouse painting is a clear memory from my childhood, but I didn't know what it meant to my mother until much later: She had etched her nightmare into that painting. Years ago, I asked her if she still had it, if she knew where it might be. She said she remembered it, thought it might be in the attic somewhere. Her indifference to my inquiry again proved her unwillingness to let me in.

I write things in order to make sense of them. I wonder if my mother was doing the same thing with a canvas and black ink. And though it's not my story, I've lived with it ever since the afternoon I learned her secret. Since then, when I help her with dishes after dinner, I make sure to put the knives away, never telling her that I know, that I feel as if I'm somehow protecting her from her fear and her memories the only way I know how.

Does she still dream the same scene? Has she ever escaped from beneath the outhouse? Maybe her pen-and-ink was her reminder, her subconscious in her art. Maybe she stenciled the way she saw herself. In pieces. Discarded. Buried.

Unlike my own mother, I grew up in a stable, sober home. It was important to my mother to protect me from the shadows of her own childhood, the darkness that threatened any encounter with her mother. Because of that, our visits were limited to Thanksgiving and Christmas, even more so as I grew up. Visiting my mother's parents meant the growing smell of coal as we approached East Texas on Interstate 30, the tension in my father's blue Monte Carlo, the obligatory weight to the afternoon.

When I was very young, my grandmother still cooked. We'd walk into the house and find the kitchen counter full of hot pads and casserole dishes simmering with vegetables. I have only one memory of my grandfather: He'd sit in the den, awaiting our arrival and smoking a cigar. A thick man who didn't hug. He died in 1976, when I was six years old. Even when I've come across pictures of him in family albums, I remember him only as a distant figure, off in a corner, sitting in his chair.

During those early visits, the hours were dominated by talking women: my grandmother and her two sisters, Aunt Dovie and Aunt Minnie. Dovie's husband had died before I was born, and Minnie had never married, so the two were each other's companions. Collectively, those three women must have smoked a carton of cigarettes per visit. The house had ashtrays at every turn, showcasing smoldering cigarettes that had just lit the burning ones dangling from the fingers of each woman. But it was only my grandmother who drank, and after Dovie died Minnie quit smoking, leaving my grandmother isolated in both of her addictions. And though she became the only smoker in her house, to me it seemed like there was as much smoke as there had ever been, as many cigarettes as always; even the array of ashtrays on every end table and kitchen counter was the same.

At Christmas, everything we took home with us smelled of the heavy smoke that had seeped in over the course of our stay. Even the letters that continued to come from my grandmother until shortly before her death carried that smell, the thick smoke of her loneliness.

But during those early years, her house was full during the holidays. Aunt Dovie's son, David, and his family, Aunt Minnie, my mother, my father, and I, all of us invading a home for a pageant of what turned out to be pretending.

The house on West Seventh Street was a dingy green, and we'd park in the black gravel drive and knock on the back door leading to the kitchen. My grandfather's red 1952 Chevrolet truck never moved from under the carport. No one ever used the front door, the one with a strong, silver bolt lock. The house had hardwood floors, and grandfather clocks lined the walls, the hallways, at least one large, carved clock in each room of the house. My grandfather collected them. They were not synchronized, so an hourly chime was more a cacophony of tones overlapping and echoing for several minutes. As the years went by, sometimes the chimes made more noise than all of us sitting in the living room together, as silence came to be the dominating chord.

A strained care was taken with words and steps through the dark hallways; I emulated this behavior, even though I had no idea why I should. I took very still baths in the claw-foot tub on evenings when we'd dare to spend the night. My father and I always stayed up long after everyone went to bed. He and I had an unspoken camaraderie during those visits, as outsiders to a history we respected by ignoring its ugliness. Even though my grandmother always kept a room that she called "Jill's room," with the most comfortable feather bed and pillows, I never liked sleeping there. I'd hear footsteps, voices, clinking noises during the night, and yet I knew that those noises were things better left unmentioned. I often worry that I'll end up in a house like that, where people are reluctant to visit and I spend most of my time sitting in a chair, smoking one cigarette after another and drinking alone. Most of all, I wonder how far

back the alcoholism goes. Was my grandmother the childhood victim of such silence, as I was? Are we all destined to
repeat the patterns of the women who reared us? Might Indie be destined to drink, like me?

I did not go to my grandfather's funeral. I was too
young, my parents decided, so I stayed at the house with
a distant relative, picking up bits and pieces of the details
of his sudden death. A dropped phone in a hotel room. My
grandfather's heart giving out on him. There seemed to be
a consensus among the family that my grandmother's addiction and behavior led my grandfather to his early death
at fifty-eight; when Dovie died a few years later, Minnie
blamed my grandmother again, warning my mother to be
careful for fear that the pattern would continue. I wondered
how a woman's drinking could cause the early deaths of
those who loved her, but through my own addictions, I have
an idea. And from what I know now, having pieced these
things together the way I always have to when it comes to
my mother, it wasn't until after my grandfather's death that
my grandmother's drinking really excelled. Maybe it was
always so bad. Maybe he concealed it for her, from everyone, or at least made the calls to inform my mother that
she shouldn't bother coming after all. Without him there to
make the call or assess the situation, our visits only ended
abruptly or didn't happen at all.

On one visit, my mother went in through the back door,
as she always did, to make sure my grandmother had remained sober enough for the visit. The calls she made ahead
of time were just another check, always an assessment of

my grandmother's sobriety, or lack thereof. Now I can see how such calls might have been a prompt, a trap my grandmother couldn't escape. On some days, she'd start drinking at the thought of our impending visit, which is what must have happened that afternoon when my mother came back out in tears and told my father, "Go home." That was all she could get out before breaking into sobs. As usual, we drove home in silence.

When I was about ten, my grandmother moved to a new, much larger house on the corner of South McMinn. I'd sit on the black and beige couch, sunlight coming in through the stained glass of the front door, a thick layer of smoke floating through the room. Once my grandmother moved, she rarely cooked, or if she did, she complained or apologized about how the food didn't turn out right. Therefore, many afternoons we'd avoid such scenes and preempt a dangerous mood with a plan to eat out. My grandmother insisted that my father take her for a drive in her four-door, maroon Oldsmobile 98. She'd collapse in the back seat, smoking during the entire drive, all the windows rolled up. On our way we'd drive over to pick up Minnie, and she'd slowly get into the car and add to the suffocating air. Minnie was a very small woman with a severely hunched back, usually wearing gray slacks and a sweater, most often in some shade of purple. She had a big smile, and every year on my birthday, she sent me a $5 bill.

Early in my life, my grandmother always dressed well and had her hair freshly permed, her tight curls dyed brown. As her drinking progressed, she let her hair go; it became a gray, frizzy mess. Her dark coral lipstick disappeared, and the whites of her eyes yellowed. I have a picture of her in better days, a handsome woman. Not really feminine, but strong, no sign of a debilitating drinking problem in her smiling face, her clear, brown eyes. She loved jewelry, and in the picture she's wearing a pronounced brooch and large ruby earrings. Rubies and garnets were her favorites, along with a few diamonds, everything gold and ostentatious. She told me once that when my grandfather called the shop where she worked to ask her for a date after that night at the dance, she first told him: "I'm not going anywhere with you." Eventually she did, and with all of his land and cattle, my grandfather offered my grandmother a good, but lonely, life. Was she drinking then? What made her drink? Did anyone ever try to get her help?

I must have been about ten the first time I ever saw booze in my grandmother's house, when I opened a kitchen cabinet looking for something to eat and found shelves lined with Budweiser cans. I quickly shut the door, not wanting to tell my mother what I had found. I can't remember ever seeing any bottles, any glasses, even when I snuck back into my grandmother's bedroom, looking for evidence. My grandmother often made visits to her bedroom during our visits, making them appear as if they were trips to the bathroom, even though there was a closer one down the hall. My mother later told me how she'd actually often drink right in front of us, from a plastic tumbler full of her favorite liquor. That's when we'd leave, she told me, when my grandmother got so drunk that she could no longer pronounce her words, or when the only words that were left were the mean ones that struck my mother like blows to the heart.

By the time I was a teenager, our family gatherings could have passed as silent retreats. The truth was that no one had anything to say. Our family had disintegrated either through death or distance, and we were no longer a large extended family gathering for holidays. We were a daughter and a husband, dutifully accompanying my mother for an obligatory visit. Looking back, the strain was cause enough for everyone to drink. No one spoke, no television or radio, just the one remaining grandfather clock in the living room, ticking, the pendulum swinging freely, the way I so desperately wanted to be, but instead we all sat there in silence. Why? Someone might ask a question here or there, but conversations never started from it. Minnie would be mad at my grandmother, or my grandmother at my mother. No one even pretended to avoid it; the silence was too sharp to dare its edge. So we sat for extended hours of smoke and random coughs. I'd follow a certain curl of smoke from my grandmother's cigarette across the room and marvel at how unlike a family we seemed. Or maybe it was as close to real as a family can get.

Minnie died in 2000, and my grandmother has been gone since 1997. I haven't been back to the little East Texas town since shortly after the funeral, but if I ever get over that way, I'm going to take her the bottle of Jim Beam I found in her closet. With that I can give my grandmother what she could not live without, what the death certificate didn't claim but everyone knew. I remember reading the word "pneumonia," and something else I can't recall, when in reality she drank her body away. She drank most of the people in her life away. Especially my mother, whose childhood dreams threatened her with her own death, who grew up with just one doll, who received money rather than gifts. I often think that this must be what drives my mother's desire for people to know what she wants, even though she doesn't voice her needs.

Instead, she keeps the secrets of her life and her disappointments to herself. How can she expect anyone to know what she wants? Or know how to avoid the remnants, the result of the inevitable letdowns?

My father has always maintained that my mother has never told him about her childhood, just that it was a hard one. Maybe he doesn't want me to know. But more likely she's really never told him. Much of this mystery, I believe, has kept my mother childlike, though I'm not sure anyone but my father and I can see it. She falls into crippling crying sessions unexpectedly. Her sobs are too deep and wounded to be caused by the fear of a sudden storm or the pushing of a boundary that she might try to blame it on. She curls up into herself. We do not touch her, and perhaps we should, but she seems somewhere too far away, too far in the past, to reach. She's spent a lifetime keeping it all so private, and so we respect her with silence. Maybe we'll discover someday that we did it all wrong. Maybe I'm suspecting that now. But if you've been kept distant for so long, how do you know how to come closer?

My mother is fifty-eight now, the same age her father

was when he died. And as successful, strong, and independent as she appears, as much as she wears bright colors and holds her head high when she walks, I find that I have a stronger urge than ever to just put my arms around her and hug her hard. As I've grown older, and especially now that I have my own daughter, I have initiated more physical overtures. Now when I visit, I'll see her on the couch and lean down and put my arms around her, or just pat her on the leg. I don't say anything, but I hold on longer than she's comfortable with, until she pats me on the shoulder with her long, slender fingers, her way of saying, *That's enough, now.*

I feel sorry for my mother, though I can only search the edges of that pity, since the sorrow comes from things I will never know about. I feel sorry for what she carries and remembers. When I was eleven she told me that if I turned out to be an alcoholic, she would blame herself, because she'd have passed on the gene. I remember feeling scared, like alcoholism was some disease I could catch, whether I ever drank a drop or not. Yet there's so much more to alcoholism than a gene—and it is, indeed, a disease. I learned in rehab that yes, I am predisposed to drinking because of my grandmother, but I can't blame or regret that she's where I came from.

More than anything, I have to make a choice about how far I'm willing to go with my own drinking. How easy it could be to lose everything, to end up like her. Could I be capable of creating the same mother-daughter dynamic I cringed at all those years? I have a mother who never knew her own mother, and perhaps that's why she could never really know me; but for all the openness I have with my own daughter, could my addiction eventually override any attempt I make to overturn my family's pattern of distance? And yet, for all the trouble my mother and I have endured with each other, for all the distance and the determination we both have to be kind to one another, for how different we are, for the hours we sometimes sit in silence, unable to think of anything to say, I don't blame her for the times when she didn't know how to love me. No one taught her how.

4. The Ones Who

> I am thirty-five years old, and it seems to me that I have
> arrived at the age of grief. Others arrive there sooner.
> Almost no one arrives much later. . . . What it is, is what
> we know, now that in spite of ourselves we have stopped
> to think about it.
>
> —JANE SMILEY, *The Age of Grief*

I am learning how to live. Not by the long-range futures I
will never know, but by moments when I choose to change
or not to. For years, I've read in the tub: Carver stories,
poetry, books borrowed from lovers. Years ago, I read the
Dorothy Parker line "I do not like my state of mind" in a
tub lined with vanilla candles. A second-story apartment in
Lubbock, Texas, furnished by my married lover. The line,
along with the pattern, has followed me, or I have followed
it, because I am a woman who likes to sleep with other
women's men.

I don't seek them out; I don't hang around faculty parties and flirt with the professor whose wife is out of town;
I don't scout for wedding rings or spend the whole night in
a bar making eye contact with the man who smiles at me
while his girlfriend is in the restroom. I don't even think
about it. It just happens. I've tried dating available men,

but I get nervous, feel an impending trap or ennui creeping behind every minute we spend together. I seem to want only the men who are taken. But after nearly ten years of balancing such freedom with forced restraint, I have tired of my mind, my patterns, my predilections, and some days, even my passions.

Recently in my life, I loved a man who called me from the walkway leading up to my house one night. He wanted to come in, to stay. "I'm already here," he called from behind the front door. And suddenly, I was exhausted by the assumption that he could come by anytime, call anytime, but I could not do the same—drop by his house, call him at home. It was as if I were sleepwalking, the way my mother and I both used to, when someone would turn me around. I'd never know what I might wake to, it reminded me of not being in charge and relying on someone to rescue me, to even know that I had wandered. So instead of answering the door, I turned out the kitchen lights, locked the back door, turned off my phone, and pretended to go to bed, even though it took three hours before I could turn my mind down enough to consider sleep.

I thought about the previous weekend we had spent together, the bookstore he took me to, the enchiladas he made on Saturday night, the cigarettes we took turns taking drags from, the way he shaved and we talked while I showered. I was playing house, like so many women in their early twenties like to do as a way to convince themselves they are grown, or at least able to finally fulfill an anticipated role without having to stay for the final act to discover that the reality of many couples reflects George and Martha from *Who's Afraid of Virginia Woolf?* more than Howard and Marion from *Happy Days*. I have seen too many Georges and Marthas, have played both roles myself, so the transience of a weekend visit or a long evening suits me just fine.

Then why, I wondered, as this man and I drove back into town and he answered a call from his wife that he ended with "I love you," did I shudder at the knowledge that our weekend together had been illusory? Why did I turn my head and look out the window—knowing that when I got home to an empty house, feelings of loss and self-betrayal would follow me from room to room as I unpacked the jeans I wore on Friday night, the camisole I slept in, the coconut lotion he liked so much? As we pulled into the driveway, he briskly told me to remove any signs of myself from his car. I felt like an illusion. Made to disappear.

He hurriedly carried my bags into the house, and then he was gone, again, back to his own. These thoughts finally won over my attempts at sleep and forced me to throw back the covers and sigh, roam through a dark house with the consideration that he might still be outside, waiting for a light or any sign that I'd given in, once again. But there was no knock on the door, no car parked outside, and the lack of his need for me echoed as if through a canyon carved by all the men before him. And the truth: I am temporary.

I suppose it was a surprise the next day, or maybe not, when I recited the line Annette Bening uses on Michael Douglas in *The American President:* "Maybe things would be better for you if I just disappeared for a while." I've always been drawn to the way lines from films can so accurately portray my own sentiments when it comes to my relationships, as if there are no more original thoughts, reactions, or responses in my head, because I've been there too many times. I get to the place where I have nothing of my own left to say, and I'd done this too many times to believe that anything I could say or do would change *him*. If things were going to change, I'd have to do it. It sounds easy, but try to let go of the one thing in your life that makes you feel that good. And then remember it's also the very thing that makes you feel that bad. I was brave enough to say, right before he hung up, "Leave me alone." Though I hoped he wouldn't take too long before calling back or coming over to say, "I'm all yours." And even that response, which I crave and think I want, makes me feel like I'm holding my breath, like suffocation. But I want to breathe—to be known, not hidden.

For the past few weeks before that night, I'd been trying to figure out how it all happened, how I ended up on that disaster train with frequent stops and no destination. I remember the first married man, how brief and insignificant our fling was, more a fascination. I didn't wake up one morning and decide to sleep with one of my professors, to meet him later in a motel room. In my mid-twenties, I discovered that the only boundaries that exist in this world are the ones we create for ourselves. Until that point, I thought life was more rule-bound than it turned out to be for me. I started sleeping with one of my professors. Then I was sitting in another professor's class one day, thinking how I liked his hands and the way he talked about novels, how I'd like to sleep with him, too. Suddenly it was as if all the doors on that boundary-ridden world I'd known were blown wide open—and a pattern was born.

In *Straight Man,* by Richard Russo, which happens to be about an English professor, the main character decides that "the truth is we never know for sure about ourselves. Who we'll sleep with if given the opportunity, who we'll betray in the right circumstance." This is a truth I now know too well, one that opened up a door to a world I never knew was there. Almost ten years and more than ten men into this gig, I have lived for far too long between what I wanted and what I thought I *should* want. What I thought I should want overshadowed what I wanted so much that I never considered the possibility of having something different.

I know too many people who have fooled themselves into thinking that their lives are not their own, friends who tell me with longing, "I'm not living the life I thought I would." But no one is, and that's the way it goes, and it's not always a bad turn in life that brings us to where we are right now. I don't know any of my friends who dreamed of being a professor or a CPA or the manager of a telemarketing firm from the age of five. None of us told our high school counselors that our goal was to rack up in school loans what could have been a down payment on a house, and none of us believed we'd ever be anything but happy—until we weren't anymore, until half of us got on antidepressants, until we realized that happiness is not as easy as the Peanuts Gang promised in their song "Happiness Is," what with that business about two kinds of ice cream and telling the time. As adults, two kinds of ice cream can be the only company we keep during an invasion of depression or the threat of an extra pound. And time is something we wish we had never learned, and we certainly don't know how to tell it, for it tells us. Happiness, for adults, is as fleeting and surprising as a waiter dropping a tray in a restaurant.

So, we create things to look forward to: the after-class cigarette, the drive to a remote place that feels like an escape, the glass of wine after dinner, the out-of-state trip to spend time with someone we trust. We live for the fleeting moment. When I was in college, I had a literature professor who loved Wordsworth, loved the idea of "though nothing can bring back the hour." I sat in the front row of her class because I found her face and hand gestures fascinating, and I wanted to be as close to what she had to say as to how she said it. One day she pointed to a robin on the windowsill of the science building just before it flew away. "Fleeting moments," she sighed.

At the time, I looked at her quizzically; I thought maybe she was a bit distracted, or a closet ornithologist. Fifteen years later, that moment haunts me, because I realize that the moment—that bird, that class, the year I did too many drugs and lived in a blue apartment with a girl named Cindy—it's all gone. And what of all those other moments I have repeated over a period of years—the hotel rooms, the surreptitiousness, the phone calls that end because she walks into the room, the leavings? Do they not stack up against each other so heavily that each time I repeat the pattern, the present is burdened with the inevitable? That what is happening can be only what happened. That the real relationship I have is with waiting. And why continue to contribute to such a collection of coming and goings? For me, it seems to go back to the fleeting moments, the sudden happiness. It's how I first loved a man, my father.

Because my father was a high school football coach, he seemed to live at the field house, dropping in at home for the occasional dinner, maybe a shower, always at least one side of *Waylon and Willie*. I'd ask my mother to leave the hall light on Friday nights after games. I'd huddle down into cold sheets, trying to stay awake, listening for the back door. Eventually I'd wake up to the sun in my room, the hall light off, my father already gone, up early Saturday morning to plan for the next week's game. My mother, like most, used the words "your father" as a scare tactic in disciplinary moments, though she admitted years later that my dad felt he saw me so rarely that he would rather our time together be good, fun. And so he'd take me to the mall parking lot during snowstorms and do figure eights in his VW Bug, or inside to get an Orange Julius. He took me to basketball games, where I'd play under the bleachers; to the curb after a rainstorm to race popsicle sticks; and, when I got older, to the symphony and musicals, meant to make up for his extended absences, his calls from the field house to say, "Start dinner without me." Thus, I grew up with a man coming and going, his stays brief but always fun and without consequence. That was how I learned to love men.

In *The Age of Grief,* Jane Smiley writes about middle

age as a time to consider what life looks like. It's a frightening moment when you "have stopped to think about it," and it's not for everyone, as Smiley says. Some of us never get there, but for me that moment arrived in 2006, when I was thirty-five. It came when I was able to identify the patterns established for me, the patterns I have chosen to follow, or not chosen to break. Also, I know who I am, what I am, and beyond certain patterns, I know my habits, my addictions, the things that will eventually ruin me or drive others crazy. I am a college professor, a mother, a wanderer, a distant person. I am ritualistic, fearful of confrontation, a runner, a heavy drinker. As for my eventual demise, I envision either another stint in rehab or another very angry and betrayed woman in my front yard. And during my mid-thirties, when I had finally gained the courage and the self-worth to sit down and admit it, I knew why F. Scott Fitzgerald's *Great Gatsby* heroine, Daisy Buchanan, called the thirties the loneliest decade.

When I am in these relationships—yes, I can call them that because they're the only kind I truly know—I get to have my cake and eat it, too. I get to be loved and I get to be left alone. I get laid, get letters, get the ache in my chest, get to keep my life as it is and as I want it to be. That means sleeping on whatever side of the bed I want to; watching *The Bridges of Madison County* on a Wednesday night and again on Friday; talking on the phone to my friend Jason for three hours at a time; drinking the last beer in the fridge;

taking off on a Monday morning and not coming home until five-thirty without telling anyone where I've been; making cookies and dancing to Aretha Franklin with my daughter and her friend; and reading as much and for as long as I want. I can even have sex with someone else if I want; after all, I shouldn't be expected to remain faithful to someone who's being unfaithful *with* me, should I? Though when I open up to someone, love someone, it doesn't matter where he stands in his fidelity to me or some other woman. I love only him, and though I've tried, he's the only man I want to or can be with. A curse, considering my choices in men, though perhaps it all comes down to this: I never want to get married or share a space with a man. I am only good at loving someone from a distance. It's the in-between I love. At least that's how I console myself.

The only problem this time is that I'm the only one in the ring, and I'm having trouble standing through the first round.

The One Who Was Indicted

"You may think you know who you're dealing with, but believe me, you don't."

—*Chinatown*

She first heard about his arrest when she got to school that morning. Called into his office, she sat with some of his other students, listening not to a confession of what he had done, but to his admission of not being the man everyone thought he was. She wondered how he could have been arrested and already back at school, how the university had allowed it. She wasn't sure of anything anymore. He even invoked that line from *Chinatown,* the one at the end of the film about not knowing who you're dealing with. She realized she knew only a few things about him: He played golf; he was the tallest, thinnest man she had ever slept with; he was the only person she knew who actually put his clothes away in the drawers of hotel rooms; he brushed his teeth in the faculty restroom every day at around one fifteen; and he liked to wear his black T-shirt often because she told him it reminded her of a photograph she had seen of Robert Redford. In that office, on that morning, she kept trying to get him to look at her, but he wouldn't. She wanted to ask him with her eyes something no one else in the room knew she had the right to ask, *Have you cheated on me?*

The last time she had spoken with him on the phone, he had told her he loved her just as his daughter walked into the room. He was always taking risks, taking her to his house, to conferences, into his office after class and kissing her; showing up beneath her balcony on a Saturday while his kids were at swimming lessons. It made her uncomfortable, skeptical, but she had nothing to compare it to, didn't want to seem inexperienced or ungrateful. She'd call down to him from the from the balcony, invite him in, fix him strong coffee, and sit beside him while he cried, the white cup shaking in his smoke-stained fingers. All she wanted was for him to leave, but she had already invited him into far more than she had anticipated. *Obligation,* she thought as he poured another cup of coffee.

After she graduated and moved north, he wrote her a letter with a Rod McKuen poem in it, something about getting little sleep, about little cure for what her absence had done to him. She had had no idea—all those Wednesdays eating lunch in his office, a box of Ritz crackers on the shelf above his desk. The first time she'd seen him, he wore Op shorts, a T-shirt, and flip-flops to class. She had had no idea that professors could be so casual, comfortable. She liked him immediately. And two years later, when he called to ask if she wanted one or two hotel rooms for that conference in Vegas, she put her hand over the receiver and drew a loud breath, knowing that all of the emails and Thursday afternoon phone calls were exactly what she had hoped they might be.

She remembers walking the Strip with him with what she now recognizes as a feeling of self-betrayal, of pity toward his wife, whom she has never met but saw once at a department party. She slept with him that first night in Vegas and every night and morning they were there, though she went out onto the balcony while he called home. And when they got back, she allowed him to come over on Tuesday nights after class. Respect for a relationship that undermined her own presence, coupled with a lack of respect for institutions like marriage and constitutions like self-esteem. Looking back, she recalls a sick feeling in her stomach every time, a feeling not that it wasn't right, but that there was something not right about him, although she couldn't have known that then. Women know this all too well, this experience—of not knowing how much we don't care, or how limited our love is, until we understand that we don't have to be with someone just because the opportunity presents itself.

She will not say it was a waste of time. She will not say she regrets it. Still acquaintances, they see each other about once a year at literary conferences. In greeting, they hug and look at each other with a knowing distance, understanding they will not pursue a conversation beyond this hello. That day, when she walked out of his office with the other students, she went down to the first floor to smoke. They did not speak for six years. It was only after she had survived far worse situations that she found the courage to forgive a man who knew long before she did that he was never worth it.

The One Who Walked Close to Walls

> "There goes the dismantled."
> —DJUNA BARNES, *Nightwood*

She thinks about that man in Alpine, the one who kept Diet Dr. Pepper in his refrigerator in case she came over. She has always remembered the smaller gestures, like the years when she loved banana Laffy Taffy and he brought some with him when he picked her up from the airport, as her welcome home. She kept the wrapper on her bulletin board for years, until it finally got lost, she assumes, in one of her moves.

He's the one who lived in a white house off Highway 10, the one who found his dog in one of his coworkers' yard, the one who knocked on the door to find his wife on the student's couch. Lanky with black shoes, he carried sorrow so heavily behind him that he was late wherever he went—to work, to band rehearsal, to his house when she was waiting for him. He never apologized for being late, as if he owed no one anything. She thinks of him now and again, when she reads poems about birds or makes the pasta he made for her the night they came back to his house high, hungry. Seashell pasta, alfredo sauce, capers, pine nuts. She makes it now when she finds a new lover or when she's feeling lonely— or sometimes both. It's the only thing she really knows how to cook.

He told her she was fun to have sex with, that there had never been fun or laughter or good conversation before her. She smiles when she remembers this, remembers the light from the street corner shining through the blinds in his bedroom, remembers him feeling her face in the dark for tears and saying, "You have a big heart."

The afternoon he came home after finding out that his wife had been fucking his friend, he broke all of his wife's sculptures, smashed them on the back patio. So surprising from this man who played harmonica and told her that she looked lovely. When he said this, she knew that she could have him, if she wanted, and she did for a while. She writes him a letter years later. "I remember you fondly," she writes. She wants to add the last lines of a Raymond Carver poem: "I am thankful for you, you see/I just wanted to tell you." But he's a poet, already has books of lines behind his desk. She remembers a slow dance on hardwood floors, cantaloupe on Sunday mornings. A man who needed to hold on to her until he was strong enough to let go.

The One Who Says He Aches for Her

> "But you I feel no distance from. Every move you make feels like I'm traveling in your skin."
> —SAM SHEPARD, "YOU I HAVE NO DISTANCE FROM"

On the morning he makes her breakfast, he wears no shirt, only jeans. As she tries to remember when a man last made her eggs and bacon, he says, "I feel like we've had sex and woken up to have breakfast." She doesn't say anything, but she's sure she doesn't feel that way. Even though it's been a long time, she can still remember what her body feels like the morning after she's completely let go with a man in her bed in the dark. A man who's put his mouth and his hands all over her. She misses this, especially when he comes into her house wearing a black leather jacket, even when he brings her wine from the state he lives in, even when he dances with her in the living room at four o'clock in the morning, and especially when she can still smell him in the house hours after he has gone.

Maybe she's been living in Utah for too long; her friend Jason jokes that she is having a "Mormon relationship." She shudders at the accuracy of the statement, though she knows that all the beer bottles in her trash can this morning would not pass any bishop's inspection. It took her six months to realize how much she thought about him, looked forward to seeing him, checked her email, wore certain clothes and colors of lipstick when she knew she would see him. He is younger, but wise. Guarded, but sure. He admits to her that he writes her questions, her sentences, down as soon as he reads them, saving her words from the impermanence of an email. Sentences like one she wrote after he told her he had spent a year in prison: "When people tell me what they have done, I say, 'Oh, okay.' It's what they haven't done that makes me *ache* for them." He wants to keep them, to remember what she said.

He likes the way she uses the word "juxtaposition," the way her laughs mean different things. She likes the way he moves, feels as if the rhythms of his body could easily be laid down on top of hers and they would move together, the way her hand does when she puts it out in the window of the car while driving down the highway—smooth undulations, a movement she can give in to easily, letting something guide her for a change. And she feels as if she could let this man take care of her. That's most significant. She feels that even though he asks her to explain herself, it's not because he doesn't understand; it's that he likes to hear what she has to say. She does not worry when he is away, or that he can only stay a night at a time every other week or so. He says they both know the other is always there. He sends her songs, she sends him books. She listens to the songs as she goes to sleep, wishes he were next to her instead of that other woman. He is the man who made her see her patterns. And in her angry discovery, she wanted to stop chasing someone else's man, or at least stop sitting around in silence.

One night she hangs up after delivering an ultimatum. But she calls back, knowing she can't follow through, and that she's too old to be hanging up on people anyway. Eventually she will find the courage to say, "I am worth more." She has never used those words, never thought them or even considered how they might apply to her. She has been living man to man, hiding, never questioning her choices. "We are the choices that we have made." A line she keeps hearing in her head, a line from a film about a woman who loves a man who is not her husband.

For the first time, she realizes that she has never asked any of the men to make a choice, and she's not asking now, either. She never would, because she wouldn't know what to do with a man if he came to her door and said, "I'm all yours," anyway. Probably shut the door and open a bottle of wine and pretend she didn't hear right, though she has a fantasy about a man knocking on her front door during a rainstorm and doing just that. She tells him that she deserves more. In fact, she says it more than she has to, not that she wants him to know it. She is telling herself.

When he calls to say he misses her now, when he calls at one o'clock in the morning to say he loves her, when he calls just after midnight to ask if he can sleep next to her and she says no, she can rest easy. She can get up in the morning and know she has been good to herself. She will not give a man everything he wants. She will let him do that for her, and if he does it right and long enough, she might just let him in when the rain comes.

The One Who Took Her to Mexico

This weight
on the other side of the bed
is only books, not you.
What I said I loved more than you.
True.

—SANDRA CISNEROS, *LOOSE WOMAN*

He calls her on a Thursday to say he will be in town on Saturday, this man who asked her if she wanted to go to Mexico three hours into their first date. He meets her at the bar where she waits tables, a dark place with martinis, velvet couches, a bartender whose favorite writer is Truman Capote. She wonders for two days why he has called after all this time, why he is coming, this boy she dated during her first year of a doctoral program, a boy who took eight years to graduate from college, a boy who said his favorite thing was coming in to find her drinking wine and who cried the night before she left town, asking her to stay, admitting he hadn't been there for her, whatever that means.

She moved back to Texas, because all the boxes were packed, the apartment already rented. She didn't hear from him, didn't expect to, until months later when he called her to tell her his dad had left his mom, after thirty years of marriage, for a twenty-five-year-old woman. She felt guilty, gripping the phone in the kitchen where her married lover had pushed her against the refrigerator just hours before. Guilty for being the very thing that had caused his father to leave, she forces the similarity out of her mind and counsels him through months of anger and stubbornness, and they learn they have a good friendship.

"We should have left it alone after Mexico," she always tells him, though she doesn't believe it, and now it seems, ten years after Mexico, neither one of them has ever truly left it alone. When he first contacted her, she thought about that night they left the Wormy Dog Saloon, a bar on Washington, when he told her, "When I get a good job, I'm going to ask you to marry me." But now he did have a good job, and he was planning a wedding to a flight attendant from Houston.

They had been a fun and dangerous couple, hitting the Wormy Dog at least three times a week, driving down to Mexico and back to Oklahoma over four days, traveling in a van with seven other people to see Jimmy Buffett in Kansas City, and getting so stoned they couldn't remember where they had parked the van. They drank Tecate, ate chicken quesadillas, his favorite, and rented *Urban Cowboy* about once a month. She even started calling him Bud; he called her Sissy. Yet, like many college seniors facing graduation, he worried that staying together would hinder his chance at a life glorified by naiveté. So he stopped coming around, stopped answering the phone. She'd run by his apartment in hopes he would see her, see his mistake. Once, a few years back, when she went to visit him in Dallas, he had the *Urban Cowboy* poster in his bedroom, the one she'd given him before she left Oklahoma for Texas.

When they were in school together, they thrived on their common penchant for going to strange places, pretending to be something they weren't, convincing strangers in faraway bars that they were newlyweds or investigators of some recent incident in town, which always got someone talking. The last time she'd seen him, after he had been married for a few years, they'd met for lunch. He made overtures, so did she, because it's hard to not be honest with someone you've loved and lost. At one point, he told her that during his drive to the restaurant, he wondered, like so many times before, what his life would be like if he were with her instead. He had decided nothing. He could not be any happier or any more successful because of his choice in a woman. She thought about choices, changes we're all too afraid to make, how we assume that something else will never be better than what we have, or how even if it is sure to be, we choose to ignore it, so in the end we choose nothing. We let our lives, our situations, choose us, and we are taken in, helpless.

Once again, she left him in the parking lot, wondering if he felt the way she had the night in Oklahoma when she sat on the bottom step, waiting for him to come back to his apartment. Wanting something and knowing whatever it was wouldn't measure up to the nights she lay in bed and imagined it. But it's the knowing that they might have had something else in life—like each other—that has kept them together. In May 2005, he died unexpectedly from an enlarged heart, and even though a mutual friend called just hours afterward, leaving just his number and an urgent request to call, she waited an entire month. She wanted to ignore the truth for as long as she could, even though she knew it already. She felt him gone.

The One Who Went Away

> I felt no feeling of fatherhood.
> —ERNEST HEMINGWAY,
> *A Farewell to Arms*

It's her daughter's third birthday, and she is taking down the bed that was once a crib. Her sobs echo in this small room, though she can't figure out why she is crying, knows that it's about more than this girl of hers growing up. It's not that she can't name the thing; it's that there are too many things. She removes the sheets, asks herself questions, though it's not an answer she gets, but a snowy night in March.

A week after her daughter is born, she and this man move into a cheaper apartment a few blocks away. She liked the old apartment, where she could write at her desk while he read in the brown chair. Now she stares at the space in the carpet where the chair used to be, remembers how he cried quietly as he read the ending of *A Farewell to Arms*, telling her he wished he had never read the book because it made him realize what it would really be like to lose her.

She had a cesarean, so she does not help with the move, but stays at the old apartment, cleaning out the refrigerator, pulling out all the condiments and cold beer, the tasteless shakes they have for breakfast and lunch because they are so broke, and putting them into the cooler. Sweeping the kitchen carefully, she looks over at her baby in the blue infant seat, feeling like he's not going to come back to get them. When she opens the front door to sweep out the dirt, she does not feel cold, though thick snow falls in diagonal lines, the glow of the streetlight making the night seem both magical and haunting.

This apartment is empty, except for the cooler and the vacuum, which she cannot push. She cleans the bathrooms last, leaves toilet paper, something she does in every move as a gesture to the next tenants. She wanders the rooms of the apartment, remembering how she much she likes the creek that runs behind their back porch, where they eat cereal together in their lawn chairs on mornings when he has the day off.

She feels lost, alone, as if she already knows what is going to happen. When she hears the U-Haul outside, she goes to the door, hands their daughter to him, and mops the front hallway before leaving the mop leaning against the doorframe. It's the middle of the night, still snowing, and she's taking her daughter home, following the U-Haul through the snow, the streets thick with sludge and slickness. When she steps inside the new apartment after a slow and careful trip up three flights of stairs, she finds all of the furniture in the living room, as if he has given no thought to how she will move the bed, the nightstand, the bookcases to their respective rooms while he's at work tomorrow. She stands in the middle of the room, rests against one of the bookshelves with her daughter asleep on her shoulder. It is after midnight; one week after giving birth, after thirty-three hours of labor, she is beyond exhausted, but there are things to be done.

He's over six feet tall, almost three hundred pounds, with curly brown hair and a thick goatee, and seems invincible to her at times. He never really seems a man; he's more a giant. Tonight he stands near the front door behind a pile of boxes; in three months he'll be gone. She hates to ask, especially after he's been moving in the snow all night, but she wants the crib assembled in the front room, where, on a not-too-distant night, she will stand at the window, waiting for the blue of his truck to pull into the parking lot. She will give up around 5:00 AM but find him in the brown chair when she gets up two hours later to nurse the baby. She will know. For she knows too well the look of a man who is thinking about someone else, the voice that changes on the phone when someone walks into the room, the way a man acts when he is obligatory with his time. She will not fault him for leaving her; she feels she is due.

She explains that she will sleep on the floor; she wants the baby to sleep in her crib and feel safe, as if nothing has changed, and to not know that they had to move because they couldn't pay rent and one of their cars has now been repossessed, or that this man, her father, is impatient and anxious. She asks again, angry at her helplessness, at the painful scar, the pain medication that keeps her in a daze, the depression she has no idea will grip her in a few weeks and render her a stranger. He grumbles, puts the crib together. This night is where her thoughts have been as she takes this same crib apart. She cries, feeling good and wondering why she hasn't taken this out of her daughter's room before. She cries for the three years already passed, for the little girl she celebrates, for the way she no longer feels alone when it's just the two of them.

The One Who Gave Her Words

> The young woman he left her for was in his D. H. Lawrence seminar, and since then he's taken up with a Brontë woman and a Joseph Conrad woman, before finally coming up a cropper with Virginia Woolf.
>
> —RICHARD RUSSO, *Straight Man*

Maybe that's why he stayed with her for so long, because she was a Kerouac woman, a Bret Easton Ellis woman, a sex, violence, and Western woman. After they had been together for a few months, he told her about the Willa Cather woman, about the hotel room they slept in across from her husband's law office. It was as if he guided women to study, write about authors he loved as some kind of intellectual jerkoff, a voyeuristic critical fucking. He signed his comments on her essays with the word "Excelsior."

She loved to listen to him talk in class, wrote down words he used in the margins of her notes: "inchoate," "adroit." He told her months later that the first time she stayed after class to ask him a question, she moved toward him and he did not step back. He drove home in his red Dodge Daytona, thinking about not stepping back, about bringing her closer. He ate dinner that night with his wife while he looked past her and out the window, wondering if he could have one last young lover. At sixty-two, he could fuck longer and better than he ever had in his life. He no longer worried about getting to the climax, though she would beg for Friday to come faster so that she could seven, eight times, until she laughed for him to stop, convincing him she had nothing left, even though she masturbated as soon as she heard the screen door close behind him.

He had bought many of the things in her apartment, like the beige rug she stepped on each morning as she got out of her empty bed. The hardwood floors of the apartment were cold in the winter, and she often had to sleep under three quilts to stay warm in a place with only one heating unit. She lived across the street from a pay phone and a parking lot, and the entrance to her apartment was in the back of a house with rickety stairs and chipped white paint. She loved her solitude, but back then she struggled with living alone while the man she loved slept in a bed next to a woman who brushed her teeth and handed him a towel as he stepped from the shower. She told herself each Friday that it would be the last, but their time together would restore her somehow, even if it just packed away the loneliness for an afternoon, the way sweaters get stuck in the top of a closet for the summer.

Who knows how we end up in the rooms we do, saying things to people we'll never see again after another year or two? The first time they had sex, he had gotten a room at the Holiday Inn. She was underneath him in a series of rooms, 236, 125, 245. Then afterward, she listened to his words about distance in his marriage, understood his inability to move away from it. He'd take quick showers, rinsing off the scent of sex and the vanilla lotion she wore. After a month or two, he came to her place instead. Such sustained secrecy breeds dangerous bravery. He parked his car in the garage, stayed an hour and a half, sometimes two, taking his clothes off with the sanitary order of a doctor visit, draping button-down shirts, khaki slacks heavy with a belt, white underwear, and socks carefully over rocking chairs and couch backs. No wrinkles allowed. No smells. No mussy hair. Same quick shower. He'd fold his wet bath rag on the sink, and she would leave it there sometimes for a week, pretending that she shared a life with someone.

At ten past three one Friday, something purple caught her eye in the back yard. A woman pushed the wooden gate open. She held her breath, watched the older woman walk over to the garage, peer inside, then exit the way she had come. She watched out the window until the purple trench coat disappeared down the alley. She called him, warned him not to come. She was tiring of interruptions of things she shouldn't have been doing to begin with.

But just as she began to grow weary of the suspicious glances in the hallways and the convoluted plans on Fridays, he seemed to lean toward her more. His need unsettled her, and the closer he came—needing more than wanting— the more she withdrew. This time it was she who felt the need to step back. He seemed to need two worlds in order to survive, as if watching the six o'clock news with his wife was bearable only because he had the smell of her on his fingers. She finally came to understand that this distance had been the attraction for him, while for her it was about standing at the living room window alone on New Year's Eve, while cold rain fell on empty streets and *All About Eve* played in the background, and somewhere across town confetti fell between her lover and his wife.

He liked to take her for drives to small West Texas towns and eat at Dairy Queen. He liked to leave notes in her mailbox or under her door. Slips of papers with words like "miss," "thinking," "last night." They shared blue eyes and a birthday, the novels of Cormac McCarthy, but he did not want to share the mundane, the quotidian, one of the many words he taught her. He did not like the fact that she drank so much, and he refused to talk to her on any night when she had had more than two glasses of wine. He said she used words she wouldn't mean tomorrow. He could tell, while the friends she went out with on weekends had no idea, that she stared at salt and pepper shakers to stop the spins. One night, a friend told her that her lover had taken up with yet another fling. She acted aloof, offered something from that book she'd been reading by Richard Russo, how "rumors are the manna of our particular desert."

When she was safe behind her front door, she screamed for a while, and then cried while she listened to the tapes they had made together, an exchange that began early in their relationship. He would tape a song, and after she listened to it for a few days, a hundred times, she would tape one for him. She still has those tapes, likes to listen to the arc of their relationship now and again. Now that she can truly hear it, she hears how she was asking for more and he was answering, *This is enough.* The morning after she learns of his new romance, she goes to his office and fakes tears. The truth is, she's relieved. She has ducked rumors for too long, slept in hotel rooms alone, abandoned in closed-curtain darkness with white sheets, white bath-rooms. She has watched people talk rather than listening to them, wondering all the while if he's left an email telling her when they can meet again.

She tells him that she is hurt and sad. She feels that three years should warrant some kind of right to instill guilt, though inside she knows that she has finally been let go from something she couldn't stop herself. How difficult it is to estrange ourselves from routines we wish we would not follow. She remembers the "S" he signed at the end of all of his letters, the green ink he preferred, everything he gave her—most of it words: the alphabetized books on his office shelves, the postcard she sent from New Mexico taped to the wall behind his desk. She keeps one of his books on a shelf in her living room, pulls it down every once in a while and opens it, listens to his voice.

5. Li(f)e

Janey Pearson loved owls. She decorated the living room of her house, the walls of the hallway, even the bathrooms, with owls: ceramic, macramé, watercolor, even the thick yarn hangings that were popular in the '70s. My father would sometimes call her "The Owl Lady," and other times "Cat Woman," because cats of every color came and went through a small door in the back of the house. I remember the color of yellow gold, but that could just be the color of the early '70s in my memory.

The Pearsons were friends of my parents. David coached with Dad at a high school in Mesquite, Texas, a suburb twenty miles east of Dallas, and Janey was an art teacher in the district, like my mom. David used to do this thing with his face that I loved. I'd climb up on his lap and watch intently as he blew up his cheeks and switched the air from one side to the other. Fascinated by such magic, I begged him to do it every time I saw him, stumped by how he moved the froglike balloon from one side to another in an instant. The other thing that sticks out about David is the silver can of beer he always had in his hand. I felt comforted by the sour smell of his breath and his dimples, his dark hair and constant smile, the way he laughed, in almost a cackle, and the way my father laughed when he was with him. And I liked Janey's hair—long and black, just like Cher's, who was singing with Sonny every Saturday night on our TV.

Twenty years after the nights in that owl-filled living room, I returned to Mesquite to teach high school English at the school where David and my father had coached as young men. I was right out of college and unwilling to think there might be a life outside of Mesquite, Texas. In the tradition of small towns, David had become the principal of the school, though the Pearsons and my parents hadn't remained the close friends they had once been. I'm not sure what changed in those years, but I suspect that alcohol had something to do with it. Though my father drank when I was young, he grew increasingly stern about not being around anyone who drank, or close to any place that served alcohol. His reluctance seemed more judgmental and discriminatory than anything, as if anyone with a beer were two sips away from immorality.

Meanwhile, David had become known for hosting faculty parties at his house, and at the one he had in late August of 1992, the Coors was traded early in the evening for Jack Daniel's, and he consumed enough to make everyone uncomfortable. Though I didn't attend, I listened to the stories with curiosity. Gone was the easygoing beer-or-two man of my youth. And in listening I had another thought: *Where was Janey?* No one ever seemed to mention her, and I could imagine her standing at the kitchen window, looking out at a life she didn't recognize.

For whatever reason, it almost seemed as if Janey

didn't exist that year, as David walked the hallways of the high school with a shiny bald head with remnants of his dark hair on the sides, his frame a bit thicker all over. He dressed impeccably, in slacks, a tie, and an always-crisp white button-down with a bright pair of suspenders. He was still handsome, but there was a coarse edge to him now, almost an anger, and when I'd see him walking the halls he seemed to have no recollection of a fascinated little girl, a can of Coors, the ease of a Saturday evening spent in a living room listening to Jefferson Airplane. He seemed determined in his professionalism, and I wondered if he ever thought about those years, or if he preferred not to associate me with earlier times. Being naive, I assumed that what we had once been must disappear, as if it had never happened. But at times, I would wonder, *Did he forget, or am I supposed to?*

I taught high school for only one year, and I'm sure that David had something to do with that. Though he remained a nice-looking man, the easy laughter and comforting persona were gone, replaced by a thickness seeming less like extra weight and more like an entity that weighed on him, as if a force of impossibly heavy proportions threatened to erupt and those suspenders were like bungee cords, keeping it from breaking loose. There were rumors that the new male Spanish teacher from a private school in Dallas had been hired to replace the attractive female one because of her affair with David. I didn't get as many details as I might have liked, since the teachers dropped the subject once school began, the way I dropped the instinct to ask David to puff his cheeks when I'd see him in the lounge. He had turned into an unpredictable man, and I suffered his histrionics with the rest of the faculty: emergency faculty meetings at seven forty-five; his climbing up on a chair to yell about lunch duty or leaving school before four o'clock. At first I attributed it to the coach in him, gathering his team in the locker room before the game, but his rants were accusatory and oppressive, not motivating.

The man was not happy. One day he'd pass me in the hallway and ignore me; on another day he'd smile and ask how my dad was doing. He acted like this with everyone, and all the teachers got in the habit of asking each other, "Which Mr. Pearson is here today?" I steered clear of him as much as possible, though when I had to go to his office for one reason or another, the door was often shut or empty, and both felt suspicious. I remember having the distinct feeling that his office was off limits. Ten years later, I heard that Janey was in that office on a Saturday afternoon and found an email from another woman, but I was in graduate school three hundred miles away by that time.

When I turned in my letter of resignation at the end of that first school year, it was with a sense of relief, as if I were escaping some kind of dungeon where everyone avoided waking the dragon. After learning the truth so many years later, I now understand why a man would be so quick to erupt, so elusive one day and ebullient and carefree the next: He was living a lie. He was in love. But not with Janey.

During that teaching year, I was still dating my college boyfriend off and on and spending Thursday through Saturday
nights in country-and-western bars, dancing with strangers
who all held a beer bottle in one hand while two-stepping
me around the floor. I was as close to my boyfriend as I was
willing to get to any man at that time in my life, meaning
that I was happy to press against him on the dance floor or
in my bed after the bar closed, but as soon as the sun came
through the blinds in my window, I wanted him gone. I was
restless and young, and I had no idea that people like Janey
were suffering in ways that I would soon come to know. I
was at that age when love might be found on any weekend
night, when we're so convinced of our opportunities that we
don't limit ourselves to any one man.

At that point in my life, I was always just a phone call
from getting laid. I had no experience with sustained love,
and little investment in conversations my boyfriend started
about marriage. By the time I heard about Janey and those
emails ten years later, so much had changed, as it should
with time. And while I hadn't seen or spoken to Janey in all
those years, I felt as if I knew everything about her life and
her heart.

Janey's discovery of David's secret life was the catalyst
that brought her and my mother close once again, and my
mother, perhaps sensing there was something of a moral to
Janey's story, told me all the details during a visit home not
long after Kenny, the father of my daughter, had left me.
I understood Janey's need to confide in someone who had
known her during earlier years, someone who could assure

her that yes, her life with David had been good once. She spoke with my mother regularly, via telephone and email, about what she knew and when, about how she was spending most of her time at her sister's house since it had all happened. I recognized and empathized with the addiction to heartbreak, something that plagued me for far too long; you see it in the way a person is always wanting to voice it, to support its longevity, by wondering what and where things had gone wrong.

According to my mother, David asked Janey to go to his office one weekend to get some paperwork on his desk, and when she got there, his computer was on. Closing windows, she came across an email from a woman who taught economics. The message was not about school. The "accidentally open" email is also how one of my good friends discovered her husband's secret life, and so I have decided that if I ever run across an open email on the computer of a man I love, I'll quickly close the window and go on with the laundry or the book or whatever it is I'm doing. But then again, maybe I'd be too curious, too distrustful, not to check. After all, if you don't know, does that make it any less real? I'm sure Janey had sensed a distance or an indifference in the bedroom, across the kitchen table. And I know from experience that ignoring distance is a feckless strategy. I'm sure she stood in that office, putting the pieces in the places where she knew they had gone all along.

Judging from my own relationships, and from the experiences of my women friends, men who want out act out. They come home at seven in the morning. They leave emails open and purple bras under the bed. They don't want to confront; they want to be confronted. And they live by this truth: An omission is not a lie. They compartmentalize life and switch realities with the closing of a door or the answering of a phone. David went through years of such duplicity.

He had his speech rehearsed and ready, though it was barely tactful and surely unnecessary. He told Janey he had never loved her, thus wiping twenty years of her life away in one afternoon. What David had been doing all those years was something my father calls "carrying on." My father swore he had no idea. No one did. The longevity of their surreptitiousness amazed me. David and Janey had one son in college, so when David walked out, he left Janey alone. My husband left when our daughter was four months old, and during the early years I often felt that her presence pronounced my loneliness, my solitary nature as her only parent. I imagined Janey walking through a house she had shared with the man who told her he'd rather not be there anymore. Not having been in their house since 1978, I don't know if owls still peered from the walls when David told Janey that her life, their life, had been a lie. In one afternoon, she discovered that so much had not been what she thought it to be. But how can you let go of something that's already gone, especially when that something is everything?

During my visits to my parents, we'd pass the house where Janey's sister lived and see Janey's car in the drive. My father would slow down, as if we were passing the scene of an accident. Janey had bought a new car, which

I applauded, but I also wondered how it could not serve as a reminder of David's leaving. I didn't have a car when Kenny left, and he called one night to say that one of his friends would sell me his car for a good price, and Kenny would take on the monthly payments. I wanted the car but I didn't want to be indebted to Kenny. Instead, I borrowed the money from my parents and drove to the friend's house, where I handed him cash and he handed over the title. That exchange yielded a beat-up, rusted Subaru with no heat and no defroster in the middle of a Colorado winter. Every time I drove it, I felt as if I were driving the embodiment of my life. Janey seemed to have faired better with a new Passat. Still, I thought it looked sad in the driveway. Surely twenty years has more trade-in value.

I hadn't spent twenty years with my husband, but when you commit yourself to living a certain life, and then the person you're sharing it with tells you that he's not going to let you have it, I'm not sure the number of years matters. I never think of the time with Kenny as wasted, because it's not the years I want back, it's my heart; and I suppose that after having a life with someone for twenty or thirty years, there's a lot of heart missing. Each time we'd pass and see Janey's car, I wanted to stop and get out, to go into that house, sit down next to her, and hold her hand. I wouldn't even say anything. Being left is a country with its own language—one of silence, shame, guilt, questions, pain, longing, wondering, self-deprecation, and admission, finally, that you did see this coming, but you never imagined it would actually happen. Sometimes you just mess up the sheets and comforter on that side of the bed so that you don't have to look at it for what it is: empty.

When I first heard David and Janey's story, I struggled to reconcile what a life is, because their lives together had been a lie. Unbeknownst to her, Janey was a front for the secret life her husband was living. So what does that make her life, if not something not real? Her not knowing that she had a right to go out and find her own life was the omission David perpetuated for far too long, and that was the real lie, because you can't share a life with someone who's living his with someone else.

I wonder if David ever wishes he could step back into his old life as easily as he used to switch the air from one cheek to the other, maybe because I wonder too often if Kenny ever thinks about the blue house on Stover Street, the chair where he used to read by the window, or how he used to sleep as close to me as possible until I asked him to scoot over, when he'd mumble about not wanting to be far away. I wonder how long we hold on to what was, no matter how long it's been since it disappeared or was taken. It's one thing to hold on to memories; it's another to hold on to a life that turns out to be just a part of a life, and to live like a solitary resident in a ghost town. I wonder if Janey feels like I do, like life has turned into something like owl collections or two-stepping, just something we once knew well.

Seductions

6. On Longing

If I ever meet a man who says, "You'll never want for anything," I'll pick up my purse, pay for my two glasses of chardonnay, and call a taxi. For two hours now, I've been staring out the window of the café. It's that kind of day—gray, still, cold—when I wonder if I shouldn't have just stayed in bed, or at least in my pajamas. But on days like this, I like to take books I've already read to a corner table in a cozy café, preferably in a bookstore, where people tend to show more respect for quiet. Today, it's *Door Wide Open*, a collection of letters between Jack Kerouac and Joyce Johnson, written in the two years following the publication of the infamous *On the Road*. It's a revealing exchange between a young woman never satisfied in love and a weary man crazed for the next moment. But I'm not reading. Instead, since the moment I sat down with my latte, I've been staring out the window. I know better than to sit next to a window. Not because there's a draft, or because I get too caught up in people-watching, but because I have a tendency to long, to court my sense of dissatisfaction. And longing, for me, usually occurs next to windows.

There's a Spanish film called *Central Station* in which a woman, in the final scene, sits on the bus as it departs and thinks about leaving, about what she's going back to, where she's been, and where she'll never find herself. Throughout the film she never articulates this, until her final line: "I long for everything."

I used to rent *Central Station* as a catalyst for falling down in my own melancholy, but now I'm too afraid of what reading that subtitle might do to me. As I get older, the things I long for are broader, harder, and not just a door knock or a credit card away. Most days, it's the kind of longing Joyce Johnson talked about in one of her letters, the "longings we [can't] yet articulate." She and Kerouac had that in common, except that Jack believed in the power of geography, and he should have paid attention to one of his own literary predecessors, Ernest Hemingway: "You can't get away from yourself by moving from one place to another. There's nothing to that."

In my twenties, I lived a life promoting the opposite idea, driving to faraway places in hopes of escape. Two trips punctuated every year for me—Boquillas, Mexico, in October and Bottomless Lakes, New Mexico, in May. When the smell of fall first blew into Lubbock, Texas, I'd start imagining wood smoke, the drive through the Davis Mountains, the chasms of Big Bend. And as girls started showing up to bask in the sun at my apartment complex's pool, I felt myself moving west, dipping my toes into the cold waters of that New Mexico lake. One year I realized that the problems I carried with me every day in Texas had been transposed onto those foreign, yet familiar, landscapes, and when I returned home I cogitated about the immediate re-appearance of my problems, which caused me to ache once again for the freedom of unknown territory. I had a difficult time reconciling why I couldn't bring tequila and mud tacos back to my office in the English building. Why those two worlds were so far apart, and why I couldn't keep the idea of Mexico without being there. I stare at a line in *Door Wide Open*, when Joyce urges Jack: "Stand still for a while and don't run. Things are worse when you run from them."

I consider how I've been working at staying in my life, working to stop longing to learn the streets in a new city. I think of Kerouac, who fought the desire to go with a need for solitude, who tried to convince Joyce that she, too, should not harbor fantasies of a life outside herself, in a country or a city far away: "In fact your salvation is within yourself, in your own essence of mind."

I do believe that most of what constitutes our longings comes down to distance, though not the kind recorded in numbers on the side of the highway. For most of us, there's a dangerous trap of space between what we have and what we want. In *My Father's Daughter*, Frank Sinatra's death was described by his youngest daughter, Tina, as an escape. According to her, her father left her mother, Nancy, for Ava Gardner in 1949, a year after Tina was born. But Sinatra never fully removed himself from his family, and during all the songs and women and shows of his life, he carried two dimes in his pockets to call home every evening to talk with his children. Here was a man who crossed the distance, who dared to imagine he could live a different life, though later he realized that he wanted both—a family and the freedom to love other women. Tina wrote that once he left, he never felt "safe or whole" again.

If you wonder whether this is true, all you need to do is sit down and listen to Sinatra sing. He was hurting every day of his life. Maybe that's why Kerouac liked him so much, alluding to him in his novels as he did, because Kerouac himself wanted to settle down. His mind was on the wife he couldn't live with, and interaction was the mistress he craved as he suffered to watch the "days, weeks go by and nothing said," a line from his novel *Big Sur* tracing this particular struggle.

Kerouac's salvation lurked in the corners of city streets, in the escapes from his mind to someone else's through the riffs of a stranger's ramblings or the all-night conversations between his friends. But after a while, he'd hear the words of his friends as the babble of a river, and he'd want to go away, to be alone. Then, when alone, he'd itch to get back to his friends. Fleeting peace or a fleeting connection? "What binds us is invisible," he writes in *On the Road*. And what would silence him would prove to be even more illusory, as alcohol threw a fire under the feet of his demons.

Through the years, I've struggled with the choice between isolation and connection, but most of all my desire has always involved the idea of *somewhere else,* or wanting what is not there. Men. Or desert landscapes. Or a better job. I know I'm not unique in wanting more, in missing what I used to have or what I've never known, but I do think I'm part of a group of people who refuse to ignore those longings. Some people have never run off in the middle of the night or made the phone call at whatever cost.

To me, that kind of longing—longing within stastis—is more threatening, though I can admit I've known that as well. And through the years, my drinking eclipsed any other longing I might have. I am intimately familiar with being overcome by the notion that all I longed for was my next glass of wine. Still, my thoughts return again and again to what I long for besides that drink, and, like the woman in *Central Station*, I long for everything. At least she's on a bus when she says that; Joyce Johnson is sitting in a cabin with the ghost of a man she is still clearly in love with after all those years. I don't blame her. I understand her, especially when she writes: "The trips I didn't take . . . have always haunted me."

I remember when a friend's son was three, she worked to alter his "I want" statements to "May I please have?" So if he blurted out, "I want hot chocolate!" she responded, "How do we ask for things?" He made a face, sometimes jumping up and stomping on the floor in frustration. After all, it's difficult to discover obstacles to desire. Finally, when he mumbled, "May I please to have hot chocolate?" he was quickly rewarded with the desired cup of it, overflowing with marshmallows.

Their exchanges raised questions for me. How *do* we ask for things? Can it be as easy as syntax? I've always been convinced that our needs become more complex as we get

older, but I can remember the force of that little boy's longing for hot chocolate being as strong as my own for solitude,
as essential to survival as an annual trip to Mexico. I suppose the distinction comes in how long we harbor that longing. I cannot recall my friend's son spending the afternoon
staring out the window at the empty driveway, ponder-
ing the hot chocolate he didn't get on a Saturday morning,
though I've caught myself many times staring off into the
distance, thinking about the things I can't or don't have.

Now I am staring at the Brakes Shop across the street,
wondering if there's a man in there who's kneeling down to
check brake pads and yearning for more. "Yearn," a word
that lingers as heavy and slow in the throat as it does in the
chest. Or maybe that man has no idea that there is more.
I see longing in the eyes of most people, like the crossing
guard I pass on the way to school each day. Sometimes, I
want to pull over, motion her to climb in, and offer her a
ride—as John Steinbeck puts it in his own travel narrative,
Travels with Charley—"away from Here." I want to offer
her some kind of *Thelma and Louise* insistence on not taking it anymore. Each day as I drive slowly past her, I wave.
She knows.

Window staring gets me nowhere. I know this, which
is why I know better than to position myself here. And it's
not that I really need to *go* anywhere, though for some I
think it's imperative. There are levels of unhappiness that
become unacceptable when prolonged or ignored. For those
people, if it means filling out a change-of-address form at
the post office, here's my pen. For me, I already know that I

will move to a different city, a different state, sooner rather than later. And my state of mind will pack its bags and put them in the U-Haul, right next to my wobbling television stand. Okay, so maybe on this move I'll finally lose that TV stand, but I don't want to lose my capacity for longing, for missing, for wondering what might be, for yearning for what has come, gone, or disappeared before I had a chance to save it. What I want is both far and near, or even out of range, and the distance between all of those could be one night or one year or never.

For me, not knowing what's next keeps my possibilities open. The people walking by the window, staring at me staring out, can't begin to imagine the things that I've longed for: longer legs, a man to buy me a beer and never ask me what my name is, my little girl to always want to spend time with me, a glass of chardonnay, a weekend getaway, electrolysis on my eyebrows, a phone that rings when I'm ready, to run into Robert Redford in a restaurant, to wear only matching panty and bra sets, to always be looking forward to something, to stop replaying conversations in my head, to learn how to make lasagna, to read *Don Quixote*, to hop a train and see where I end up, to get back to Mexico in November, to take a nap and not worry about what time I need to wake up, to know where I'll be in five months but never know what I might be doing in twenty minutes, to find that rock along the Poudre River *and* the one along the Rio Grande, for Sinatra to sing the next song on the radio, because "nobody cares like Sinatra sings." Kerouac wrote that.

7. My Two Countries

The borders are not secure. Highway 385 South out of Big Bend National Park leads to the Rio Grande, the border between Texas and Mexico. When you get close, you can feel it. The farther you get down toward Mexico, the quieter the world becomes. After thirteen miles, you'll come to a dirt parking lot that backs up on brush, and then a clearing that leads to the bank of the river, where worn men wait to take you across the border for $2 in boats that were once aquamarine but have now—with the murky current, the soles of cowboy boots, the summers of flip-flops—faded to a gray reminder of their original color. Two bucks and you're in a different country. No passport, no ID check, no one guarding the borders, only the tired-eyed oarsmen slowly pulling you into foreign territory, like some kind of dark gravity. A place that feels like nowhere.

Boquillas del Carmen is a mile into Mexico, but there's really no road, just sandy ruts and the cracked, gray, flat clay of a landscape marked by an eerie absence and the feeling that you shouldn't be headed toward some distant town. Once across the border, you have three choices: You can hop in the back of a pickup truck and pay five bucks to be driven into the city; you can straddle the back of a mule and ride there like some ancient vaquera for the same price;

or you can walk. It's a long mile, and on your own the direction is not always clear. Everything is flattened out here, no distinction within the panoramic view, and Texas disappeared behind the brush and fell into the canyons of Big Bend the instant you turned your back on it.

When I was in graduate school in Texas, Boquillas was a stop on an annual trip that a good friend and I took to the Terlingua Chili Cookoff at the end of every October. The first time I went was because she called and said it was emergency. For Jen and me, emergencies meant late-night phone calls and an impulse to escape. If graduate school was grinding us down or some man was letting us down, we knew we had each other, and that with one word—"emergency"—we could be out of town within hours. And when October came around, we always knew we had Boquillas.

Boquillas is a one-street, two-bar town. The bar on the left serves mud tacos, twelve for a dollar. It's an open bar, meaning no walls to close you in and a patio that hides in the back, a slab of concrete with rusted chairs and a view of crumbling adobe buildings with glimmering solar panels rising from the roofs like satellites. The tacos are small; all twelve fit on one plate. They're greasy and mysterious, and you crave them and all the accents of this city long after you have left. The late October wind bombards the city in a continuous rage. There are no barriers in the landscape to break its determination, no doorways to block its insistence, and if there is a respite, the stillness is even more jarring. There is no sound here, no music, no traffic, and little conversation, only hushed suggestions from silhouettes that lurk in the doorways and the narrow spaces between buildings.

Down and across the street, next to the troubling presence of a defunct gas station, is a white building with a red and white CARTA BLANCA sign over the open doorway, the words LICORES MEXICANAS Y CERVEZA beneath it. Barred windows on either side of the door, no glass, just open rectangles in the architecture. There's something intrusive about a building with no door, as if there is no protection between the anonymity of the street and the secrets inside. "LICORES MEXICANAS Y CERVEZA" turns out to mean tequila and warm Tecate and something called Sotol. The place is better known as the Formaldehyde Bar, for its smell. Two pool tables lean at one end of the room. Balls rolled lazily across the table either trip across one of the worn spots in the felt, or roll down the slope and hover against the side until the next stranger picks them up and tests the table's legitimacy. It's a roll that keeps pace with the movements of the bar's slumped patrons.

A chord of violence trembles beneath the surface. One afternoon, a man was stabbed on the steps outside this bar. And just as quickly as the knife had been jabbed into his belly, a truck skidded up to the steps and two men hoisted the bleeding man into the back of the truck and sped away, in a cloud of dust and confusion. For a minute, the bar became cold with the proximity of death. A shock of blackish red on the steps, like a handkerchief left behind and unclaimed. But that violence was tucked away, folded into the afternoon as easily as dollar bills into the pockets of barefoot children selling bracelets.

On most days, Dottie, the owner of Buzzard's Roost, a bed-and-breakfast just beyond town, sits right inside the doorway, like a smiling sentinel. With long gray hair and a guitar, Dottie sings a lonely song and waits for nothing. This is the life she chose years ago, when her third husband died and Texas didn't seem so simple.

Out the back door you can find a suspicious structure of three walls and a hole in the ground, while black-haired boys loiter, lean into the bar's open windows, and whisper in collusion their wares of ganja and horse rides to the Roost, both $3. You can get into a lot of trouble in Boquillas. You can get into a lot of trouble anywhere, but when you cross the Rio Grande, there's a shadow across every minute—the threat that night will fall before you can get back to the boat, and the threat that you won't want to return. Both threats compete, until you can't remember which side you're on at any given moment.

It was 2000 when I last crossed that border, and I realize how much more difficult keeping those sides balanced has become for me. Those were the years before drinking was something I hid or lied about. Even so, I drank beyond my limit on that first trip, and every other one, pushing far past the point when everyone else subsided into sips. I was still guzzling, worried I'd run out or wouldn't have enough. And it wasn't that I was afraid I'd lose my buzz; I just always wanted more. I keep a picture of myself leaning against the wall of the Formaldehyde Bar, holding a warm Tecate can in my hand. It sits on my dresser, reminding me of the afternoon I had the chance to disappear.

Now that I have a daughter and Jen has a husband, we've had to abandon our emergency calls and settle for long emails and reminiscing. But now, after all the trips, those emergencies that urged us to escape, anytime I have that feeling that I'd rather be someplace else, I think of Boquillas, the last days of October, the yearly ritual of crossing borders. Back then, Jen brought her married lover, Sam, all three of us running from the truth of our lives. Mexico has always allowed me to lie to myself, to pretend that once I cross that border, everything on the other side no longer counts. Those years I traveled to Boquillas, I too had a married lover. Somehow Jen and I had wandered into a universe in which the men we slept with were never around in the morning. They were pouring coffee into the blue cups that their wives had picked out, and shuffling the newspaper across a kitchen table. Compartmentalization, my lover was always saying to me. The separation of two lives that allowed us to live one at a time, without any consideration of its conflict with the other, except I didn't compartmentalize as well as he did. When he went home, he had her. When I went home, I had the reality of being temporary. Three years of motel rooms and circumlocution.

Though my lover never broke beyond the confines of surreptitious emails and Friday afternoons, Sam often accompanied us on our excursions, from overnight trips into New Mexico to weeklong treks along the Mexican border. He was the only man I ever knew Jen to lose herself to, and she was lost for five years, but I couldn't blame her. I remember her calling me one night, after she had taken her first job and moved out of state, to tell me that he had said he was coming to visit, but it was past midnight, and she realized he wasn't coming. That was the beginning of her being able to let him go, though it would take a few more broken promises for her to realize that she had wrapped herself up in a selfish man who did as he pleased, regardless of the consequences.

Sam fascinated me. The first time I met him was in front of Allsup's, a convenience store, gas station, and liquor cabinet in Tatum, New Mexico, ten miles from the Texas border. He was following us in his own car, and though I had never met him, I knew who he was the minute I saw him. He was every country song, the kind of man Kerouac called a "dime store Western hero." Sam worked hard at his mythology. He was a mystery in a black shirt, a sad and lost man with three children he never saw. He was the kind of man I both wanted and didn't want to sleep with. But Jen was my friend, and the three of us would steal away many more times after that first night, until my presence grew to one of detachment, a distance that would allow me to take our journeys as a solitary traveler with company only when I needed or desired it. Sam had his own distance, and some nights, when he thought Jen and I were asleep, he'd pace slowly, his boots clacking on the hard, dry canyon floor. I'm not sure he ever lost whatever haunted his mind enough to sleep.

As for me, I thought I could lose it all just by driving far enough away. Jen and I both believed that. We needed to believe that. The problem for Jen, however, was that

Sam was often the thing she needed to get away from, and those trips were the only times when they were able to be together out in the open, though I always thought those big canyon spaces exaggerated the pretense of it all. I felt sorry for her sometimes, and envious others. On one hand, I could get in my Jeep and drive away from the married man whom I had allowed to hijack my life. He'd talk about leaving his wife sometimes after we'd make love, when we'd just lie on the bed and talk before he had to go, but as it turned out, I was the only one who ever had the guts to get away. Jen had the man she wanted to be with actually with her, while I couldn't have that. And being there with her and Sam made that knowledge all the more real to me. So I'd drink or smoke pot to forget.

As Jen says, she is my memory. And because we've known each other since junior high, she has a lot of memories to keep for me. I've often asked her to remind me of things—of parties we went to together, of how I got home, of things I've said. For many years, Jen wasn't without her own predilection for getting crazy; after all, one night we racked up a $48 tab on dollar-drink night, smoking a pack of cigarettes between us. I think that was the same night we both drove home, the two of us holding on to the steering wheel of my car in hopes of avoiding swerving. But eventually Jen grew out of her drinking-past-last-call phase, and after one or two drinks, she'd abandon me in the bar as I careened toward being out of control. In the past few years, she and I have lived at least three states away from each other, and I've needed my memory more than ever.

Despite these lapses, there's one afternoon in Boquillas six years ago that stays with me. Disregarding Jen's insistence that I not buy weed from the little boy behind the Formaldehyde Bar, I did anyway, just before he offered us a horse and a ride for $2 each. Ahead, Jen steadied herself easily on her horse and turned back now and again to make sure I was coming along. That trip I rode a swayback horse toward the Roost, where Dottie was waiting with her enchiladas, her five-room bed-and-breakfast, and an endless curl of cigarette smoke floating from her lips. She offered a room, but I worried about not getting back across the border before sunset and said so. While I waited for her to finish fixing our supper, I wandered along the banks of the Rio Grande, which looked much larger from this side. I had a horse tied to a fence, a pink-robed woman making me enchiladas, and dusk hovering above the horizon. If I stayed longer than an hour, I would miss the boat. Standing on a large rock looking out over the river, I glanced back every now and again to the adobe houses of Boquillas, the longing of their pottery color, their women leaning in doorways, their children only crying voices inside. Suspended on a border with a setting sun that seemed to fall faster every minute, I wanted to make some kind of offering to permanence, so I took one of the white stones and wrote my name across it, clear and large, and placed it so that it faced Mexico. Texas was across the river with my life, but I was high and drunk enough to feel tempted to leave it there.

Dottie set down a plate of enchiladas and made apologies for her hair, which was still in plastic curlers at five o'clock in the afternoon. Her face had been broken by the years and sun, like the walls of the cantina. She smoked as the light shifted behind her shoulder, and I balanced my attention between listening to her and watching the position of the sun in the orange-smeared sky. She talked about the year she left Texas, a state that meant nothing to her without her husband, the life she had so wanted to change and which now no longer had any trace of what it once was. I thought about my life, and the man I wanted who had his own, about the lie all three of us were living by being there, how slowed down the minutes seemed, with or without the ganja. But which was the lie? On which side of the border was I truly living? Was there a lie, or was here the truth?

By crossing the border, I had created an inversion. I could see the same things—the man, the complications, the white sheets of the motel rooms—but I saw them in a different way. What I was looking at didn't change. I did. After all, wasn't I more honest, more myself, sitting there at a wooden table with a woman who was so lonely she opened up the five rooms of her house to the fleeting? Everything was fleeting that afternoon, and I knew I didn't have much time to make a decision one way or the other. I wanted something to come along and make that choice for me. The sun to set, Dottie to offer me a job, my horse to race into the open spaces where borders could not reach me.

Soon, a purple curtain began to close, its drapery folding down upon the sunlight. I felt a rush as I dared to imagine that I could have a different life. That I could disappear into Mexico. I paid Dottie for the enchiladas and the company, the chance to see the outcome of a choice I was afraid to make. I untied my horse from the fence, steadied myself on his back and turned him back toward town. For the next several minutes, I slowly raced the sun, hoping I might lose. That Mexico might win.

After September 11, 2001, the federal government established strict control along the South Texas/Mexico line, forever changing the lifestyle of border residents and ending employment for many Mexicans, afternoon soccer games between Mexicans and Americans, sunsets spent in hot springs along the Rio Grande, and an overall laid-back way of life. I have not returned. I prefer to think of the border the way it was to me then, open to possibility, free of fear.

8. New Mexico Road

There seems to be a mythology to the last minute, especially on rainy nights. At the age of twenty-five, just months after my college boyfriend Dave called off our wedding, I was headed west on Highway 6 in Oklahoma, under the navy sky of late August, toward Lake Carl Blackwell. A good friend of mine was driving me to the lake after an evening of drinking Bud Light on the porch, while I spoke and squeezed bottle caps into crescent-shaped miniatures of metal art. He told me that listening was only an idea of understanding, and suggested a trip to the lake.

I have always been willing to pick up and go, so as rain began to whisper on the street before us, I grabbed a sweatshirt and jumped into the passenger seat. Soon I began to relax, as I always do on the road, feeling that anywhere I'm heading is better than where I've been, and believing, if only for a moment, that the images I'm escaping won't follow me into foreign territory. The moon looked more like mist that night as we stood on the shore of the lake. Todd hopped up on a large rock overlooking a lake that was smooth save for sporadic raindrops, spreading circles that swelled and overlapped, searching for the shore. He handed me a rock the size of a matchbook and told me to think of the problem I had been telling him about, and throw that rock as far as I could. "Let the problem go," he said. "Throw it into the lake."

Since that night, I've thrown many rocks, though rivers are now the receptacles of my sorrows. I stand at the edge of one, staring into a rock-bottom stream in the moment before I skip, toss, or even heave a stone to forget words and images. I find just the right rock along the shore, the one I want to reflect the weight of my troubles, the thoughts I don't want anymore. I draw my hand behind my shoulder, gripping the stone and holding my breath, immersing myself for a final moment in whatever it is I want to disappear.

Out of the many rocks I've thrown, one of the heaviest has been the one for Will. I met Will in a graduate seminar on the novels of the American West when I was living in Texas and working on my master's. Smoking our after-class cigarettes, Will and I started up a conversation about the landscapes in the various novels we were reading for the seminar: Cormac McCarthy's *Blood Meridian,* Leslie Marmon Silko's *Ceremony,* and Willa Cather's *Death Comes for the Archbishop*. The readings made me yearn for the sun-soaked, jagged spaces of the Southwest. Will flicked a stub into the trash can next to the building, while I lit a second smoke. We traded off the names of bars where we'd worked, the road trips we'd taken, and the geography of our dreams. When I mentioned a little town in New Mexico, Will took an extra-long drag from his cigarette and squinted his eyes. Later, over a few pitchers at a bar across from campus, Truth or Consequences, New Mexico was the first place I thought of when Will asked me where I most wanted to go in *real life,* and I knew it was more than a question, it was an invitation.

Will and I left the next morning in my black Jeep Wrangler with a cooler of beer and sandwiches, our backpacks, my atlas, and a compilation tape that I had made of bands ranging from Willie Nelson to America. About a hundred miles into our trip, we were in Tatum, New Mexico, at Allsup's, where I always stopped. We loaded up with beer in a Styrofoam cooler. Will took over at the wheel, with an impressive capacity to time gas station stops based on how long it would be before we needed to stock up on more beer. It was obvious that he had been on this road before. I wondered if he had driven the flat road alone, on one of his fishing trips, or if he went this way with any woman willing to head west. I had no claim on Will, and something about him told me not to ask.

After four hours on U.S. 380 and most of side one of my tape, it was obvious that neither one of us was ready for a shift behind the wheel. Will knew a little place in Roswell called Corn Dogs Plus, so we designated the corn dog the official food of our trip while we tried to eat the drunk away, or at least down a notch. It was then my turn to drive, so I turned south on I-25 toward Truth or Consequences as Will flipped over the compilation tape so that Willie Nelson could start singing about the slow-moving ways of cowboys. By the time we pulled into the little desert town of Truth or Consequences, I had been driving longer than I had wanted, and what I wanted was another beer. Will had gone through one or two without me, singing the Eagles to the darkening sky. I kept thinking how we seemed to be taking separate trips together, and I appreciated that he probably sensed it, too, as he either kept pretty quiet or sang along with the different voices on the tape. I kept thinking how I was living some kind of scene out of a novel, but I was too busy drinking and getting to Truth or Consequences to think about how it might end.

We decided to get a hotel room first, and Super 8 was the only one that fit our budget. Since we were up for anything and had reinstated a solid buzz during the three hours from Roswell, we couldn't resist stopping at the big bowling alley, the Chile Bowl, we passed in our search for a room. It turned out to be nicer than we expected. A small-town, local-league kind of place, it was bright and smoky, the knocking of pins sharp and loud. It even had a bar, so we moved quickly past the large, shiny lanes and straight to two stools, where we ordered Bud Lights from the burly bartender who told us karaoke started in fifteen minutes. Will and I looked at each and laughed, knowing we wouldn't sing, but glad to have dropped in on two-for-one Wednesday.

The bartender turned out to be quite talkative, full of questions, and I kept thinking he had to be over six feet tall. I'm not usually attracted to really big men, but he had dimples that gave him an easygoing sincerity that I liked. I couldn't help wishing I weren't with Will. We could stand only two or three songs before deciding to check out one of the hot springs the bartender told us about, along with the story of the town's name. Sadly, it had little to do with truth and nothing to do with consequences. It had something to do with a television game show by the same name. I pretended I didn't know the true story and stuck to my own imaginings of a small town with a big name—how it had named itself not after a game show, but after a choice. While Will and I pooled some cash for our tab and a tip, I caught the bartender's eye and smiled. I was attracted to the character-like truth of him: a bartender in a bowling alley in Truth or Consequences, New Mexico. I knew if I ever got back down there, I'd stop in for at least a beer.

Two days later, Will and I decided it was time to head back. Truth or Consequences was hot and still, with nothing much beyond a bookstore that didn't have air conditioning, a bunch of hot springs, and the bowling alley. We spent most of our time lounging around the pool at the Super 8, keeping our buzz and reading now and again chapters in *Rocket City,* the novel we had to have read by the time we got back to class the following Monday night. When we started the drive north on Friday, we made one last stop at the Sonic at the edge of town for corn dogs, and waved goodbye to the truth and all its consequences.

Looking out at the empty landscape along I-25, I thought about the night before, how Will and I had finally agreed that it wouldn't be a trip worth talking about if we didn't have sex, but it had turned out to be hurried and based more on more mutual need than on passion. Or maybe we were just adding another element to the plot. In San Antonio we gassed up, restocked our beer and supply of salty foods, and traded drivers. After settling into the passenger seat and tapping on a new pack of Camels,

Will downed the first of our two six-packs and wiped his dark, straight bangs from his eyes. He flung the ice from the wet can onto the dingy, worn floorboard. "Don't slow down until you find an abandoned-looking parking lot and a roadside bar," he said, staring out the passenger window. I balanced the speedometer at seventy, driving away from the red rocks of southern New Mexico. It seemed that Will was talking more to himself when he began imagining the perfect tavern down the road, the one with colder beer, the yellowed Budweiser lights with the horses and carriage, the unchanged calendar behind the bar. I added the cooler covered in bumper stickers, along with a jukebox playing Waylon Jennings, or maybe Merle Haggard.

I wanted to hear "Swinging Doors," but Will assured me that "Tonight the Bottle Let Me Down" was the better ballad, as he began to bellow the chorus while pulling on the flannel shirt that he had grabbed from the back seat. I suggested a waitress named Louise; he added her husband, sweating on top of the roof, fixing the air conditioner. By the time we spotted the first sign to Roswell, we had already been there, drinking beer, playing pool and old country songs for a few hours in our minds, getting to know the locals, watching a guy named Hank lean over and assure us of his millions in mutual funds that his wife knew nothing about.

We were in no hurry; Will never seemed to be. He inspired a wanderlust I had never known, maybe because he didn't seem pleased with anything he was currently involved in, from a midnight guitar group to a recently published article on priapic imagery in the novels of Willa Cather. I had heard of his disillusionment before we had the Western novel class together. According to the department gossip, he was a promising graduate student who had accrued a wealth of "Incompletes." Although this was a man who could make instantaneous decisions and poignant observations about life on a road trip, he also seemed removed from the directions of his own life. He was sad, and I knew it. Maybe that's why he liked my company.

Later, Will told me that the purpose of our trip was to find all the side roads that others never allow themselves to go down. I wondered how many side roads Will had already traveled, the dark roads he kept hidden. It had become clear to me, after three days of being on the road with Will, that we were indeed on different journeys, our internal landscapes separated by the canyons of our private geography. I pondered the deserted road ahead, the sky taking up more space than the flatlands, the words we spoke into the emptiness around us.

Will excited me, not because he showed me things I'd never seen, but because he saw nothing strange about my penchant for picking up and moving on, for drinking in dark bars alone. The idea of not having to be anywhere surged within me, and as Will's hand brushed my bare leg in the predawn darkness, his other hand swapped out an empty can. I took a long drag from my last cigarette, blew the smoke through the crack in the window, smiling to myself and to the Pecos River. When my Jeep slowed down, I glanced over at his profile, shaded by the lurking dusk, and wondered at the man who had surrendered to complacency after a day's worth of drinking. He hummed a song that sounded only vaguely familiar to me as I passed another mile marker. Will had not noticed the river outrunning us, the gas gauge. I wondered about the side roads he had mentioned four beers back. When the Jeep finally gave up to empty, Will slammed the passenger door behind him before disappearing toward the river. Even in a few short days, I had become accustomed to and sometimes grateful for his distances.

On the shoulder of the silent road, I grabbed the leftover corn dog from our last convenience store stop, squeezed mustard onto a napkin, and then shook the renegade sips in the last beer can. Tossing my head back, I let the warm drops fall onto the back of my throat. Through the dusty plastic window, I could see Will's faded baseball cap floating above the fence that was lining the road, his arms waving. I may not have known where Will had been, and I wasn't sure I wanted to know, but I sure wasn't going to miss the opportunity to see where he was headed.

Spilling from the truck, I steadied my sandals on the gravel and steadied myself in the middle of that New Mexico highway, swirling in the morning heat of asphalt, waves of wind. Freed by the intense solitude, I spoke aloud to myself, surprised of my own voice in such vacancy: "Remember this." I, too, have my own secret spaces. Cormac McCarthy writes that the heart's desire is to be told some mystery. Mine has always been to be one.

This next part is the strongest memory: I looked down

from the ridge above the river to see Will knee-deep in the Pecos, smiling. Something about this man allowed me to act as if I were alone, as if no one would ever know, or tell, what I was doing there. With just my bare feet in the river, I took off my shorts, tank top, and peach bikini he had bought me in Alamosa from one of those all-you-ever-need kind of roadside stores, tossed them aside one by one, and waded out to where he was looking down as if it were his own private river, confessing that he'd never been near even the sound of a New Mexico stream without a fly rod.

Will did not enter me immediately, as he had the night before; instead, he cradled my head in his hands and silently lowered me into the water. He undid the barrette holding all of my blond hair, sifting the river through each strand. I knew Will was not mine, even in that moment as he lifted me up, kissing my shoulders, my neck, the slope of my stomach. His fingers traced the line of my hips and disappeared under the surface of the river, not stopping until I shuddered.

As the sunlight peeked through dry brush, he put his arms under my body and supported me as I dissolved into weightlessness. I felt good; the undulations of my sex floating, merging with the current of the river. When I put him inside me, I groaned with a satisfaction similar to the kind emitted after spotting that long-awaited gas station during a long, solitary night drive. We fought against the river's current like animals caught in unexpected depths.

I've been away too long from rivers, and there are no rocks here, only words. I'm writing to wash away the images, the whispered words that I want to forget. Some moments of our lives follow us like drops of water in a river joining other passageways, changing them forever. The memory of making love to Will in the Pecos River is not mine, it's hers, some woman who had once been on this same road with Will long before me, a woman he told me about during the last hour of our return. And I'm not sure why he even told me; it was the most he really told me about himself during the whole three days. I wondered where that woman was, if Will had ever seen her again.

I haven't seen Will since a summer night outside a bar almost five years ago, and I still carry the memory of the floating woman, the one who inspired him to stand naked in a New Mexico river, the woman who made him vulnerable enough to hope that she would join him there.

I've taken the trip to anywhere a dozen times, trips of no rush, no direction; I even took that road trip to Truth or Consequences with Will. We did smoke together on the steps of the English building, we did plan an irresponsible trip through the blurred prism of beer, and we did make it to that desert town, but the truth is that I'm haunted by a woman I have never met, an afternoon I have never known. It wasn't that I was that attracted to Will; it's that out of all the trips I've taken, none of them have had such a moment of such freedom and passion, not sober, anyway. Everything for me has been about wildness and taking chances, drunken, perfunctory fucks and forgetting. I don't think there's a man out there who could speak in such a way about me. So I'm throwing the heavy stone of that afternoon, that image, into a river that keeps following me, like the Pecos. I hope it sinks to the bottom, that the ripples spread only far enough to miss the edges, where I stand.

9. Driving Through Kansas

I'm driving through Kansas, and it seems like it will never end. All flat fields and a straight highway with too much distance between towns. Heading west toward the end of the day with the sun in my eyes feels as if I'm driving straight into the end of the world. And since Kenny left, it feels that way anyway. At first it seemed that nothing was happening, not to me, anyway, almost as if I'd left my life, or at least my heart, back at the gum-lined counter of the last Chevron. But lately I've been thinking how many pieces of my heart have been borrowed, taken, torn, ignored, or are just missing. And when I think of love and loss, I think about my friend Ann's heart, too, what part remains, how much of it has disintegrated since that Saturday night when I called her and told her the truth.

I remember the afternoon when Ann showed me where her husband had proposed to her in Palo Duro Canyon, and even though, or maybe because, he had had an affair, she lingered and spoke wistfully of an afternoon before they had any idea that either of them might ever want another. I thought she should stop the car, get out, and toss her ring right into the abyss. But she had decided many years before then that she would stick it out, though, as it turned out, she did have a breaking point. She found the email, then the purple bra (she hates purple) by the bed; and then she gave her husband forty-eight hours to make a decision.

Now that I know what waiting for someone to decide the rest of your life feels like, I can empathize with how agonizing those forty-eight hours must have been. Her husband, Steve, took his time, too. He called his best friend, who advised that there was no choice; he had a family, a wife and a son, and so he stayed. Not because of counseling and not because of a heart that could not let go of Ann; he stayed because of that call and the power of the word "family." And so Ann spent the next five or six years building back the percentages of trust. When she hit 92 percent, she felt as if life might finally steady. She stopped asking questions, said she'd rather live without asking, especially when she didn't want to hear the answers. The only answer I ever wanted to give her was, "Leave." But it wasn't my marriage, my son, my heart, and so I stood by all those years and watched her protect what she had using one simple strategy: ignoring it all. Three years later, their marriage trembled once again under the weight of a secret life. But this time it wasn't his; it was hers.

I think Ann fell in love with Tom because he paid attention to her. Ann has always held to what she calls the "80/20 principle": If you get 80 percent of what you want from your spouse, you can live without the other 20. Ann loves numbers, and Tom loved words. As she once explained it to me, "I didn't know that real-life people talked to each other like that"—the way F. Scott Fitzgerald writes. Tom loved to talk about books and films and writing, which for

Ann constituted that 20 percent. For some women, seduction comes from a bottle of wine or a burgeoning flirtation. For Ann, it came from the 20 percent.

They met at a book editors' convention, and she found him attaching himself to her, asking her questions. She found herself noting his impressions, wanting more.

Soon after the convention, the facade of his professional interest was exposed, as emails turned into instant messaging, then phone calls, then meeting for more conventions or readings, sharing a room, and eventually entertaining the notion of leaving their respective families for each other. She lived in Texas, he lived in Illinois, and soon seminars in Las Vegas, Austin, and L.A. weren't enough. When an editor position became open in Chicago, where Tom had been working for years, she applied and got the job. Within two months, she moved her family to Evanston.

Ann convinced herself that the move would be beneficial professionally and financially: She would get a substantial raise, better benefits, more childcare options, and a larger job market for Steve, which would help with the higher cost of living. I wonder about the cost of her living, about the risk she took in following a man she believed would listen to her heart, only to discover that she had been one of who knows how many. I suppose it would have been easy for me to brag about my foresight that something was off with him. I met him only once, but that was enough. I never trusted him, and not just because he had a wife and two kids at home. I was worried about Ann, and my intuition proved correct.

Less than one year after Ann moved her family to Chicago, Tom decided to enter the PhD program at a university in Texas. What struck me as most suspicious was that he left his wife and kids in Chicago, assuring them it would allow him to focus and finish his studies earlier. According to Ann, he promised bimonthly visits back home. Because I had a friend who was a professor at the university, I surreptitiously kept tabs on him, never reporting to Ann that I was doing so. I wanted to protect Ann, who seemed more drawn to him than ever. She found excuses to fly to Texas to see him, and I was increasingly worried that she would leave her family for him. Not even one semester after Tom entered that program, the chair of the English department told him he was no longer welcome. After only fifteen weeks, Tom had managed to elicit sexual harassment complaints from both faculty and graduate students. He had even dabbled with a few undergraduates from his composition course, one of them underage. Tom returned to his wife and kids in Chicago, claiming, according to Ann, that being away from them had been too difficult. He told Ann the program had not been right for him. She believed him.

I guarded Tom's Texas secret for several months. Then Ann called one Saturday, after a six-month silence. I knew the call was not about catching up on our classes, or what our children were up to, though it took her an hour before she uttered the real reason for her call. Once again, she and Tom had come up against the raging question in their relationship: whether to leave their families. When she asked me what I thought, I decided it was time to tell her what I knew. My intention was to protect her from hurting herself more. But I know the truth doesn't always matter, and I'm not naïve enough to believe there's not more to their story.

That moment I told her felt like watching something extremely delicate and expensive drop, when you wince, hoping that it won't break, even though you know it's going to. Ann stayed silent, later telling me that she felt as if all of the air had been sucked out of the room; she could feel the earth spinning. She asked me to hold on, and I heard her put the phone down. Enough time went by that I ended up hanging up. Ann called back about twenty minutes later, telling me that she had run to the bathroom to throw up. She never questioned the truth of Tom's indiscretions, said she knew he was capable of committing them, though not the underage part. Most of all she felt betrayed and unattractive in the face of what a seventeen-year-old body—one that hasn't given birth or reached its mid-thirties—must look like. She kept saying, "I feel ridiculous."

Before that phone call, Ann had a heart that had been following its seducer in a frenzy. When we hung up, she had no place to put it. In decisions involving the heart, I'd argue that no advice is ever really heard or wanted; we just need people to hear what we want, no matter how wrong or impossible. And we'll listen to our own heart over advice every time. My mother once told me to listen to my head instead of my heart, and I answered that I was trying. Plenty of people worry what everyone else will think of their decisions, their lives, and it hinders them from living the life they truly want to live. But for me, it's my heart that holds me back, even though I've known for a long time I need to be free. Still, I struggle against a heart still heavy with loss. I feel compelled to stick it out. I owe my heart that. In Ann's case, her heart had been with Tom for three years, and he didn't seem willing to give it back, so she was again faced with a choice—stick it out, or leave a large part of herself behind.

Ann gave her husband forty-eight hours; I gave Kenny a month, even though he was already gone before he ever left. Now, even though he's living with another woman, a part of him is still with me, and I'll hold on to that for as long as I can convince myself that the part I have is enough to keep him coming around, to eventually bring him back home. At first, I was sure he'd come back; after all, long before he had ever considered leaving me, I had told him the story of Steve's infidelity, how Ann had offered him a choice and his best friend had counseled, "You have no choice; you have a family."

"That's absolutely true," Kenny had said. Then. But later, during those months when I turned those words toward him, he said, "That was true for them." I often wonder why he couldn't follow that advice when it came to me, to Indie. He kept telling me that he wasn't leaving Indie, he was leaving me. Nights when I'd ask him to help out with her, he'd mumble from the couch, "I don't want to get attached." Looking back, why didn't I just show him the door? Why did I allow him room to make any choices, given the fact that he had given me so few? But then again, I thought if I went along with whatever crisis he was under-going, if I stayed out of the way enough, he'd stay. Whereas Ann's strategy had been to ignore, I had no choice but to be invisible—I couldn't think of any other way to live, be-cause change is brave, and I was not feeling brave. I was not willing to let go of Kenny's heart, and I worked to keep what I had of it until I heard him admit the real reason he was leaving—because he had found another woman, not because of the words he'd been throwing at me about how I didn't know how to love.

But recently, when I called him, as I do from time to time but never should, he told me that he loved her. Words that I had once thought would only ever be directed at me had now been easily transferred to a woman I've never seen. So difficult to fight an enemy you've never even seen. It was then I knew he had taken his heart back, because I finally felt it go from me. It would be more time, I knew, before I could take my own back from him.

I believe we can all justify the choices we've made or haven't made based on our hearts—what they need, what they want, what they miss, what they crave. I know Ann's heart needed someone to look at her during dinner, ask her about her day, and call and tell her more than the outcome of the day's given errand—that fixing the car would be $450, that there wasn't any milk in the house. Despite the fact that I told her what I knew, I'm sure her heart needs to believe that what it has felt for the past three years has been real. For when we find out that what we loved was not what we thought it was at all, do we hang on to our truth, or someone else's? I think we do both. We live with what we want to see until we're far enough away from it to see it for what it actually was.

I know it will take Ann a long time to see how she followed her heart into and through deception. And I will allow her all the time she needs. There are no easy answers to this one, and I know every question all too well. There are times in our lives when we're confronted with the duplicity of what's true and what isn't. And we make a choice—we're either incapable or unwilling to see what's what because it doesn't matter anymore, because even the lies are the truth we know, or we choose to separate out the truth, to allow the healing to begin. One choice puts us right back on track, back into the patterns we know and understand; the other choice forces us to be brave, face consequences, and live more meaningfully. Ann will need more than forty-eight hours to make her decision. As for me, I'm working at driving toward my own truth, toward facing it.

There are days when my heart feels like Kansas, though I know better than to listen when people say that there's nothing there.

10. Blue-Collar Men

I lived with an electrician long enough to learn how to hide wires. In the years when Kenny and I were together, during that significant turn from my twenties to my thirties, I watched him install telephone jacks, remove outlets, and run wire from room to room. At night he'd sneak us into unfinished mansions where he worked, revealing how open and vulnerable these homes could be without the locks and security systems they'd eventually install. We'd slowly step through each undone room, and I'd imagine the lives of the couples building these homes, the expansiveness, and by extension the distance they'd create between each other, planned into their spacious structures. As we'd walk through the high-ceilinged living areas and hidden studies, I thought about the people who would move through those doorways, never knowing this moment—how one man prided himself on how he had figured out how to get their antler chandelier to balance perfectly in the entryway.

Once, in our own apartment, Kenny worked to repair a light fixture in the bedroom. Sweating in the doorway of our cramped basement apartment, his frame seemed especially large, his tool belt draped just below his waist. It was a Saturday, and we were both home, trying to escape the heat of an early September. I sat in the next room, a turned-over novel on my lap, my thoughts pressing toward his body, trading his frustration, his concentration, for my own lust. I pretended not to know him.

He became a stranger, the electrician charging me overtime for a weekend job. At school, I always lingered around the maintenance men in the office, the hallways. I noticed the way they lurked beneath windows, carrying keys and long lightbulbs, ducking into locked closets. As an English professor, I worked in a reserved environment, so when one of these men would appear in the mailroom or approach me on the first floor, I sensed a charge from a toughness I'd never attribute to the handsome Faulkner scholar in his tweed jacket and department-issue chinos. I couldn't help scrutinizing how their shoulders hunched ever so slightly as they ascended the stairs from the boiler room, how their eyebrows locked intently as they discussed the heat problem in Morrill in serious huddles. I'd stare at the worn-down wood of their hammer handles and step my boots between their discarded tools. And now I was living with one of them, a husky, bearded man. Our front porch was perpetually decorated with his paint-splashed boots. He kneeled down in front of me, sweat pouring from his forehead. His kisses tasted salty and unfamiliar, the way I wanted them to.

We had quickly settled into a routine that included recurring fights, one of which had to do with our workspace, our tools. He had his tool belt and his tools in the back of his truck; I had my laptop. Somehow I couldn't get him to understand that he couldn't take over my laptop anytime he wanted to look up a chord sequence to

"Good Time Charlie's Got the Blues," or porn. I found myself making arguments like, "I don't just put on your tool belt or show up at your job site, do I?" But even as I said the words, I knew they didn't translate. I worked with words, an intangible trade, and I required that my writing desk be free for whenever some of those words formed that perfect sentence or an opening line. I never could convince him of my need for the privacy that any writer demands, and he never felt he had any space of his own. As much as I tried to share my life with him, I ended up imposing it on him.

Because I'm an intellectual, people often assume that I'll fall for a man who works with his mind, but I loved a man who worked with his hands. In fact, I always had trouble maintaining attraction to and interest in colleagues or bookish men. It was the sense of ruggedness I craved, the manliness inherent in a man who doesn't have to call a plumber. I loved each callous on Kenny's palms, the hardest one just beneath his middle finger. Sometimes I ran my tongue over it to taste the sweat of his work, and even though he'd apologize for its roughness, I loved how it scratched against the most delicate parts of my skin.

That September afternoon, I decided to tell him about my stranger fantasy, and I could immediately tell that part of him shorted out at the thought that I might find it enticing to see him as just some worker on a weekend call. But I insisted, showing him how excited I became at just the thought of it, and he gave himself over to my scenario, though his passion seemed frustrated, as if he knew giving in to me on this level held a little too much danger. I thought about the way his voice turned stern when he'd warn me about cords hidden beneath desks or behind beds, crossed and tangled. After that afternoon, I never asked him again to pretend to be what he already was, a maintenance man who wanted me. After all, he never showed up at my office at school, asking me to pretend to be the professor who locks her door. He seemed to prefer to not focus on how different the worlds we left for in the mornings were.

I don't recall when I began to be attracted to blue-collar men. Once, while playing pool in a bar in Stillwater, Oklahoma, I watched a few gruff-looking men in Carhartt overalls cuing up at the next table. They had come in from a camping trip, their flannel undershirts and five-day scruff more than I could ignore. For a couple of years, I taught at a university where the English building housed the maintenance facility, so I'd interact with men like Marvin, a tall, skinny man with a leathery face who was all Metallica and mullet, saving his Camel Cash to buy a neon light, which he planned to display behind the plants in his living room, sure that it would "please the ladies." There was Steve, a stocky, gentle man who liked to slow his truck and roll down his window just to call me "Sunshine"; and there was Ed, the supervisor of the weekly lottery numbers, always willing to add me to the pool for a buck. I talked easily with them and secretly loved their attention. Eventually they got in the habit of wandering by my office each morning to say hello.

That was how I got a key to the roof, by sweet-talking one of them into making me a copy, an order that could have gotten him fired. He leaned his bulky frame against the doorway of my classroom one afternoon, calling me into the hall. I thanked him, promising two things: not to get caught on the roof, and not to tell anyone where I had gotten the coveted key. When I left that university, I bequeathed the key to a colleague.

One night I met a mechanic in a bar on Indiana Avenue and took him home long enough to find out he had a tattoo on his back that he'd designed himself, so no one else would have it. There was the bartender in that little mountain town who lived in a tent along the river, the construction worker who played rhythm guitar, albeit poorly, in a country Western band, and the cable guy who stayed long after he had installed my DVR. He left his cell number on a business card, and though I kept it in a kitchen drawer for a long time, I never called.

I got hung up for a long time on a man who made me a necklace like the one Paul Newman wears in *Cool Hand Luke*, by soldering a bottle opener to a silver chain. We'd skinny-dip in his apartment pool late at night, and he'd play early Paul Simon on his guitar for me. But he called it quits, leaving a note on my door telling me I needed to figure out what I wanted. Looking back, I recognize his unwillingness to play the game I had set up, or maybe he just saw that it was a game to me. And it was: Sleeping with blue-collar men afforded me the opportunity to sink into the side of myself that loves jukeboxes with classic country music in dark bars, a rugged edge, and easy, empty conversation. That's how it really started, I guess, with periodic visits to a world that wouldn't have me in the end. Still, I worked at forcing those ill-fitting pieces together, something a good friend of mine recognized as self-sabotage.

I once went home with a man just because he said he had been reading Jack Kerouac that afternoon, which is a more respectable criterion, I suppose, than oil-stained hands. I do insist that any man I date be a reader, which is odd, considering my penchant for the kind of men who frequent Hobby Lobby more than Barnes & Noble.

Living with Kenny gave me a chance to indoctrinate my blue-collar man into reading. Over four years, I introduced him to Raymond Carver, Ernest Hemingway, F. Scott Fitzgerald, J. D. Salinger, and the poetry of Sharon Olds, among others. We'd sit out on the back porch or lie in bed, discussing the latest work he'd read with the intensity of a grad school seminar. When he'd go on the road, he'd take a novel with him. Once, he read *The Old Man and the Sea* and became so fascinated by its conflict that he spent a graveyard shift reading passages to another worker. The guy asked to borrow the book, and after that it got passed around the entire crew, each man equally captivated by that whole man-versus-nature thing Hemingway does so well. When Kenny shared with me how I'd indirectly turned a group of nonreaders on to Hemingway, I felt like I was saving the world, one refinery worker at a time. When he was home, he'd tag along to poetry readings and departmental cocktail receptions, where the conversations always hovered around our own writing or the works we were studying in class. Only then did I see Kenny as an outsider, recognizing how those ill-fitting pieces struggled against the larger puzzle.

Another of our recurring fights was over words. I wanted a man to write me letters, to leave me notes when he left in the morning. Kenny wasn't the note-writing type. Aside from suffering from dyslexia, he had a fear of writing because of it, which kept him frustrated and nearly paralyzed on that front. He once managed to write me a letter that he'd rewritten over a period of months before getting it right. He occasionally sent postcards from the road with one-liners that included fumbles like, "I'm comming home," or, "You make everything worth wile." I put them on the refrigerator, bothered that I was with a man who made spelling mistakes, yet still touched. Once, a desire to improve my own vocabulary prompted me to stick a list of words on the refrigerator, triggering in Kenny a hurt I rarely witnessed. Even though I assured him it was for me, the implication it left had already set in. I was discovering how important words really were to me, not just in my academic and creative lives, but in my love life as well.

When I got an opportunity at a different university, we moved from that basement apartment. Kenny undid all the clandestine rewiring, and it occurred to me that we'd built a home. My overloaded blue bookcase in the corner, his fly-fishing gear that leaned against one corner of the kitchen. Moving the vacuum over the carpet one last time and wiping dust from the windowsills, I wondered how anyone would ever know we had been there. All of our furniture, the blue bookshelf, the bed he called a saddle because of the way it sunk in the middle, the kitchen table where we had sipped chai and sectioned grapefruit and eaten English muffins in the mornings, the reading chair where I had cried one night after we fought as the Bee Gees blared from the stereo, the boxes of books and words I had written, all of it in the moving van as we pulled away from our beginning. But what we left there was still somehow more than what we took away. We ended up the strangers we had pretended to be, our bodies no longer knowing one another in the dark.

Sometimes when I look back, I wonder if I wanted to be with an electrician, a plumber, a welder, a man who could build fences, more than I wanted to be with Kenny. Whatever my own desires may have been, it didn't matter in the end. He wanted to leave, and my attempts were as meaningless as turning the knob on light.

The first place I got after Kenny left was also a basement, this time in a friend's house, where I ran wire from a second-level room to the downstairs, and to my computer. I wrote at the same desk he had once chastised me for stuffing cluttered wire beneath. During those first months, I spent hours spending time with words as if they were black wires, writing as if I could reroute the intricate, challenging configurations of his heart. Such disconnect, the surge of hidden wires within me, like black electrical tape woven over a white wire, tucked beneath the carpet, undetected.

I still notice the maintenance men on my campus and find myself hanging out where I think they might turn up. Sometimes I wish one would show up at my office door. All of my friends tell me I need to marry a writer, but for now, I see myself like I did years ago, the person I was when Kenny and I snuck into those unfinished mansions. When he'd show me the bedrooms with light switches on each side of the bed, we'd envision the couple as two strangers, passing the night separately, one negotiating a dream, the other ensconced in the shadow of a reading light. We could not have known then that we were describing our own fate, before we'd even surrendered.

11. Sexagenarian

It is difficult to stand outside one's desires.
—Cormac McCarthy

If you asked me to explain why I'd ever be attracted to a geezer, I might tell you it's about experience. Knowledge. Having been somewhere. Maturity. Wisdom. Sometimes, too, I describe it this way: Older men have already become what younger men promise to be. Wilbert claimed it was about not being as obsessed with the climax as he was in younger years, which would explain the four-hour stays we spent fucking on both beds in various hotels around the city. And I have to agree that was certainly a bonus, as I'd enjoy as many as nine orgasms in an afternoon before he ever considered one of his own. He liked referring to himself as a sexagenarian, though his description had nothing to do with being in his sixties. Overall, I'm not sure if my attraction was about the sneaking around, the other-woman status, the convenience fuck, or the snagging of a sophisticated, silver-haired man who loved to wear blue.

It happened that his wife began to appear near places where we had planned, sometimes only minutes before, to meet. Just as we'd find a table at a coffee shop across town, or sit on a picnic table in a remote park, one of us, usually he, spotted her blue Blazer across the street or at a stop sign. During those early encounters, we were still brave, defying her presence with a commitment to remain where we were, though eventually he tired of the charade and departed like a child called home at dusk with what by then was her signal. But her anger never surfaced—just her presence, which was relentless. I spent my time alone imagining what their kitchen looked like, whether he sat with her for coffee, which one of them took the recliner during the nightly news. Only once did she seem to challenge me, stopping alongside me at a corner in her Blazer, as if daring me to roll down my window and ask for directions. I am willing to see, only because of the distance that's developed since then, that both of them created a scenario in which they played on the same side and moved me, the unknowing other woman, across a board too intricate and complex for me to maneuver on. I had been trapped in a game without a rulebook.

We began just as Wilbert was turning sixty, and we ended when he was sixty-three. Those years were thrilling, though tumultuous, especially with his wife's suspicions following us. Like many relationships, this one began with innocuous emails. Then we advanced to a chat room. We'd type to each other for one or two hours after his wife had gone to bed, before graduating to weekly dates at various hotel rooms so as not to chance the predictability of a regular appointment. We became more daring as we went along, and moved our afternoons to my apartment, still undetected, even though his red Dodge was one of a kind in that city and was parked in my driveway for hours at a time. We'd even watch films "together," by starting a rented movie at the same time and then calling each other afterward to discuss it. His wife never failed to intercept the phone when I'd call, and I prepared myself for a stern "Stop calling here" that never came. Only now can I see that he and I fooled no one except ourselves into believing we had a purely clandestine affair, when I continually lied to friends, or when both of us denied we'd been together, even though we were careless about talking and being seen in public. Anyone paying attention or just passing by in a hallway recognizes the body language of two people in sexual collusion. And not until we were convinced that we had been discovered did we admit it, irritated at having our privacy interrupted.

The last time I met Wilbert at a coffee shop, he told me his car was packed—the "I've left my wife" kind of packed. I looked out the window to inspect his car in the parking lot and found the back seat loaded with a computer monitor, boxes, and thick stacks of clothes on hangers. Though we had often fantasized about moving together to New Mexico, I recognized at that moment that my desire for the ideal was better than the ideal itself. Imagining our lives together on my morning drives to school, or while eating at my kitchen table and wondering if he were doing the same, had been my true company. All along, it had been about the wanting, the *not* having.

After a few days of hotel living and waiting for me to meet for breakfast in the hotel restaurant where I never showed, he realized, I suppose, that he had lost both of his lives—the one with his wife and the one with me. He lived among and between those lives, never sensing that if one were abandoned, the other would disintegrate. He went back home, and I realized, like Joyce Johnson did when she finally saw Jack Kerouac for what he was, that "our love affair would be something that had happened in the past and I'd feel compelled to write about it." Or maybe the two of them just escalated the stakes, my actions proving that his wife had won that round, and that Wilbert didn't have the skills to continue in the game.

Jason often asks if that relationship was worth it. I always say yes, but maybe somewhere inside I really know the answer to be no. Yet when he asks what it was about the man that attracted me and kept me hiding for so long, I can never put words to it, a feeling Nick Carraway in *The Great Gatsby* describes as "incommunicable." I think Jason asks because he's my age, and he wonders why I kept my life on hold for a man thirty years older. For most of my friends, the married part was an established pattern, but the age part stumped them. Being with Wilbert, I quickly learned that older men are not afraid of their sexuality, are comfortable with mine, and are unabashed about attraction. No wasted time or extended seductions, no expository introductions or plot development. As Michel de Montaigne wrote, "I want a man to begin with the conclusion." I do not have the patience to wait for a man to act upon, or even claim, his desires. Older men do not pretend they are not interested.

I'm more willing to categorize my attraction to certain men by the way they look at the world. My house has areas

devoted to three men who fascinate me, including posters, film stills, books, and biographies. A black-and-white
Sinatra keeps watch over my kitchen, smoking in his signa-
ture hat inside an oversize silver frame. Books I've collected
about him line one of the corners of my living room bookcase, with several of his records stacked nearby, my favorite the purplish cover of *That's Life*. Ernest Hemingway has
his own shrine—not an altar with continuous candlelight,
but a wooden boat that hangs on the wall, the slats used as
shelves for his novels, criticism, and various biographies of
both him and his women. And Robert Redford, should he
ever walk into my house, would be overwhelmed by the images of his work on my walls. The poster from *Out of Africa*
hovers above my writing desk, and carefully placed around
the house are posters from *The Way We Were, Brubaker,* and
A River Runs Through It and a great still shot of him in the
dugout in *The Natural*. Like Frank and Hem, Bob has his
own section of books, including *The Films of Robert Redford,* along with magazines that have featured him on the
cover, like a 1978 *Screen* and a 1980 *Rolling Stone.*

Regardless of my fascination with Frank's dual existence, Hemingway's existentialism, or Redford's penchant
for sadness in life and in his work ("Life is essentially sad,"
he once claimed in an interview), many people question my
collections: *Why would a young woman like you be into
Robert Redford? Isn't he, like, sixtysomething?* Or they
focus on a December 2000 *Sporting Classics* cover with
Hemingway as Papa, or think of Frank only as "Ol' Blue
Eyes." These are the men I fall asleep to every night, and

they are all older men. But what I focus on is how they see the world, and I'm sure developing that view took years that most men my age don't have.

I can't negate the men I notice. When I'm at the gym, the shopping mall, or a restaurant, I am invariably drawn to men with silver hair. (Premature gray doesn't cut it, though I do find that very attractive.) Sometimes I wonder if I'm trying to find a man to replace Wilbert. But it's more a visceral response, one of intrigue and curiosity. Honestly, put a group of various men in front of me, and I'll go for the older one every time—unless there's a man in Carhartts or a tool belt, but that's a completely different fascination. I imagine if I ever come across a sixtysomething blue-collar existentialist with a raging libido, I'll make every move I've ever known to work.

I'm not saying that it's always been about older men. Mostly it's been about men, period. "I've had more lovers than birthdays," I pronounced on my twenty-eighth birthday in a hotel room in Lubbock, Texas. Almost ten years later, it still holds true. Though my forties are quickly approaching and I've still got an edge there, the lack of sex in my life in the past few years raises my suspicion that there's some quota no one told me about, one I unknowingly blew through in my twenties. Back then, a night out didn't end with last call; it ended when I picked up a man. Going out was a game, and I always won. If I ever grew concerned about my numbers, I'd wear my granny panties as some kind of chastity belt, though they always seemed to perform the opposite kind of magic, and I'd rush to remove them under the covers before the man of the night discovered that I had on my "big" panties. At times I slept with a man for a reason—maybe he looked like some actor on *Melrose Place,* or I thought he was a good dancer—but those nights weren't about much beyond the physical. I hope that my thirties have brought about a more refined system of choosing, though there have still been nights when I've been less than tactful, abandoning a man simply because he didn't know the meaning of the word "pensive."

I used to not be so forthcoming and directive, such as during my first experiences, which were all exploration and ineptitude. Yet one night, my own confusion about what to do while performing oral sex frustrated a young man who kept pushing my head down, so after a few too many of his insistences, I bit him. More precisely, I bit it. We were both eighteen, and the pressure from his friends and the number of beers he had downed during a rowdy game of Quarters infused his libido with anger. Before I knew what had happened to me, he threw me between a bed and a wall at a party, pinning me beneath him, slapping me and moaning, "Ooh, baby" when he felt me making any headway at escape, as several onlookers clapped and chanted from the doorway. From that day on, I made sure of two things: I would learn how to do any sexual act with aplomb and stunning enthusiasm, and I would always initiate.

I've met other women with similar mind-sets—a woman whose brother abused her with such frightening intention that she hid under her bed, or the woman raped by a first date—a story I've heard so many times that when my students write about similar experiences, I regret to admit that I respond, "It's not enough to be raped. What's unique about it?" What those women and I have in common are unflinching sexual confidence and a predator mentality. In other words, I choose the game and I go first.

The most profound change in my sexual outlook occurred when I had my daughter and realized what my body could do and had done, and I didn't feel that just any man who could keep up with me during conversation, *and* keep a hard-on, qualified. Plus, when Kenny started sleeping with another woman shortly after I gave birth, I began to question myself, and I turned my libido off for a while. Until I met Peter, a tall balding man who was sixty-six at the time, and then it seemed I was playing the old game again.

I met him at a party I attended after a poetry reading that he hosted. It was clear by the middle of the evening that he had surrendered his attention to me, and as most of the guests departed, some fellow writers and I lingered. As we all sat on the couches in the living room, Peter's friend Beverly busied herself around the apartment until Peter called to her in the kitchen, insisting, "Beverly, would you stop cleaning?" He seemed befuddled by her refusal to join us, though I recognized her silent admission of Peter's radarlike attention to me, and her act as a female version of marking territory, cleaning her lover's house in hopes that I would see clearly that she knew where the cups went in the cupboard.

She finally came into the living room and announced that she was going home, and I knew why. Peter tried to stop her, especially because she was barefoot. "Where are your shoes?" he asked, but the poor woman was so distracted by this unexpected, much younger, enemy that she claimed to not have worn any. The act of walking out the door was a surrender, but she gave a strong reminder, looking not at him, but at me: "I'll be back in the morning." And then she was gone. It had been a long time since I had played the last-one-to-leave-the-party role, but it all came back so easily, and I made it clear to the other writers that my drinking and talking stamina was not to be challenged. They eventually said their good nights, but not without some raised eyebrows at the door.

Even though Peter and I kissed passionately that night when he walked me to my car, on the last night I was in town before moving, I did not feel as much passion for him as respect. Still, respect can garner a great deal of attraction, and I do have that for Peter, though we no longer live near one another and he still has his friend Beverly. I remember feeling good about myself for not sleeping with Peter, and I'm sure it has a great deal to do with Beverly. I was, as it turned out, still willing to test my skills, but I wasn't willing to play the game. After all, I had been the woman who lost more than once, and I didn't want Beverly fearing she wouldn't be able to go barefoot in his home.

Hemingway has a collection of stories called *Men Without Women,* and those are the only men I'll consider now. Whatever my sexual prowess rested upon in the past, whether it was control, power, or a game, nothing within me now, in my late thirties, desires to do anything to a man who already has a woman, because what I've learned after sitting night after night, waiting for Kenny to come home, is that the man seems to be able to play without consequences, while the woman suffers penalties. And it's not worth it. It's probably why I've been indifferent to men for such an extended period of time.

Last year, when my frustration at not having sex for any reason finally reached a desperate level, I discovered a new way to play—online. I put an ad on Craigslist for a silver-haired man who had some free time in the afternoons.

Craigslist offers an opportunity to post listings ranging from jobs to housing to casual encounters. In the personals, categories range from "Strictly Platonic" to "Miscellaneous Romance," though I've never found a posting in the latter category because I'm sure that most people, like me, have no idea what that might entail. And because "Casual Encounters" seems to cover everything anyway, from sex to hosiery fetishes to "what I can't get at home" types of listings. What I learned, after reading the first twenty replies that came within hours of my posting, is that sexagenarians do not seem to inhabit the Craigslist sphere. Replies ranged from questions like, "Is thirty-six too young?" and, "Will forty-eight and graying but not quite silver do?" to digital photos of erect penises ("penis pics," I dubbed them). I had obviously set my standards too high for this online playroom full of lady-killers, men for entertainment, and, I must admit, occasional arousal, though I've given up coming across a silver-haired man of substance.

As a woman whose sex life has existed as a significant part of her life, it feels as if I've been sidelined. A therapist once labeled me a sex addict, though how can I be addicted to what I can't get my hands on? I am convinced that the escalation of my drinking over the past few years coincided with the weakening of my sex life, but living in Utah limited my resources to such a severe extent that I honed my drinking skills to world-class status. I knew on those long nights that were I having regular sex, I wouldn't have such an intense relationship with wine.

Note that regular sex, not a man, is at the core of my longing. And I suppose that's the core of all of it—my continual sublimation of what I want for what I should not have. I fear commitment, hence the married man who couldn't possibly threaten marriage without committing bigamy. I fear not being in control during sex, so I quickly take over conversations with innuendos and obvious suggestion. And I fear loneliness, so I drink to avoid the quiet.

12. The Space in Between

A few years ago, after I gave a poetry reading in Albuquerque, a frizzy-red-haired, black-jeaned woman approached me with a notebook and pen in hand. "I love the way you write about the space between things," she said, her voice scratchy, rough. "I've often tried, but I just couldn't do it. I was furiously writing during your reading. So wonderful how you captured that space between."

Since then, I've thought about how that woman interpreted my writing, how she understood it more than interpreted it, how she sat in that room and found herself wandering through the space that I had carved out of my own longing and feeling the familiar. I was caught somewhere between flattered and disillusioned, for I have often thought that I carve out my own unique space through my writing, and I have always considered my themes to be distance and longing. Even though she defined it differently, it felt as if my view of the world was no longer my own. I worried that what I had been writing all along had not been mine.

I began to think about the writers I admire, and I discovered something in that process. We may be attuned, but we'll never express our distance, that space, the same way. There is a thread that runs through the work I write and attach myself to, though those expressions weave themselves through various forms and find ways to give shape to intangibilities of absence, distance.

My explorations of such articulation began with poetry, when I took a workshop with Mark Cox, the author of *Thirty-Seven Years from the Stone* and *Smoulder,* a soft-spoken, stooped man with brown hair, a red wine–colored floor rug, and a rocking chair in his office. I wrote my first poem in his workshop at Oklahoma State University. It was about my boyfriend's roommate, Brooks, and his fondness for hanging out in the Wormy Dog Saloon. Brooks's mother had lived next door to Elvis at some point, and he had a picture of Elvis and his mother together in his room, along with a movie poster. His grandmother had been a famous silent film star. All of these details went into the poem, and when I talked to Mark about it, he asked why I was writing a poem about a sad man in a bar. "Ultimately, you're always writing about yourself, regardless of the subject," he said, almost whispering. He didn't buy my explanation that I hung out in bars or was sad. "But I do, and I am," I assured him, leaning out of the rocking chair. "Revise it to include you," he said. "Why does this interest you, and where are you in relation to it?" I revised the poem.

What I Remember About Oklahoma

After we make love,
I get up for the bathroom
when you tell me you love
my ass. I am tired of waiting for you

to love me better. I feel my way along
the wood-paneled walls of your apartment,
sit on the toilet with my heavy head
in my hands, moan.
On the way back to your bed,
I stop at your roommate's open door and linger
unafraid that he will see.

At happy hour, he leaned on a pool cue
in his favorite fishing shorts, his Indians shirt,
and we passed several pitchers
between us. A fuschia teddie
dangled from the moosehead
over the bar where you stood,
watching the Rangers game.
He handed me the cue, poured me a glass
and sang Waylon Jennings.

A streetlight shines through
the curtainless window
onto peeled-off jeans,
engineering notes, and two pictures:
his mother, embraced by Elvis,
and his grandmother, a silent film goddess.
I can barely see him, buried under
the rumpled comforter
as he dreams to the hum
of his window unit instead of the steady
breathing of that girl at the bar,
the one with August-colored hair
who sweeps by the pool table on her
way to the one-stall ladies' room.
He plans to tell her she's beautiful,
but when her flowered skirt brushes
his leg in a follow-me whisper,
he turns and fires the 4 ball in the side pocket.

He snores now, the man
who makes me chicken enchiladas,
talks with me on the phone
when you're nowhere to be found.

When you call from the next room,
I see you are already turned away,
ready for sleep. I wait for a moment,
stand between two doors to different rooms,
think about crawling into that comforter
instead of settling next to your back,
your face turned away in the darkness.

I had to write the poem to see that I loved somewhere between two men. The night before I moved from that town, from that stifling relationship, I let my boyfriend read it. I felt as if the poem were a confession to his fears, that I had indeed developed feelings for Brooks. Yet when he put down the piece of paper and looked at me, all he said was: "I wasn't there for you." I had never contemplated that aspect of the conflict when writing about the three of us. I wonder, then, do we only see our own location within the geography of distance? And wouldn't that ultimately leave us all in isolation, the kind that resonates after waking up next to someone when you've been dreaming of someone else all night?

I am too much in tune with the chords of distance, and so when I listen, watch, or read other artists, I am drawn to such melancholia, a chasm I fall further into when I come across the words, the images, of those who seem suspended between what is and what they want. Bob Dylan is one of those artists. And it's one particular song, "Visions of

Johanna," that caught me off guard when I first bought the *Blonde on Blonde* album. It opens with the whine of Dylan's harmonica: *Ain't it just like the night to play tricks when you're tryin' to be so quiet?*

Sometimes I can't stand it, and I have to play that first stanza again and again. Such emptiness, isolation, heat pipes resounding through rooms weighed down by a woman's absence, until everything in the room becomes ephemeral, even Louise. Dylan croons about how Louise's presence makes Johanna's absence that much more clear.

Strange how I don't feel sorry for Louise. I don't even want Johanna to come back. I just want to sit in that empty apartment and "mutter small talk to the wall" with the lights out. I don't even think Dylan wants Johanna to come back. Sometimes it's easier to love someone when they're not there. At least then no one has the power to invade your capacity to miss.

For those of us who have rambled through the hours of an evening to the dawn, Dylan doesn't have to explain himself. He explains us, the person within us who can sit on one end of the couch and drink white wine and smoke cigarette after cigarette and look at nothing but the wall, or where the living room carpet and the kitchen tile come together. It's not necessary to think of anything, really, but thoughts wander mostly to what isn't around. Such agendas of contemplation leave no chance for interruption, like a place where the phone can't ring. It's as if the melancholy becomes its own state of being, and sometimes it's comfortable, like a cup of tea or a long Sunday drive. But there's a space between here as well, because if you delve into it too far, it's tough to get out. To believe that you even can. And if you happen to be with someone who does not understand the distances, it can be devastating.

Kenny was so threatened by my propensity for melancholy that he went away. "You are too much in your head," he told me, "and you're sad." He thought he could make me happy. I never really wanted to be. Looking back, I realize that I never lived with Kenny, just as Dylan lived more with the idea of Johanna than he lived with Louise. Kenny was just something that lived beside me. Most of the time I lived elsewhere, or in a state of emotion that contradicted my surroundings, and in the end, he could not live with only part of me, especially the part that was prone to such sadness. When I look back on life with Kenny, it's not the chai tea in the mornings or the laughter in the darkness of our bedroom that stays with me. It's the distance, the nights I stayed up long after he had gone to sleep, fighting the visions of a life I wanted, the ones that clashed against the one we shared.

In a 1970 *Life* article on Robert Redford, Richard Schickel wrote, "People possessed by visions do not settle for parts of them." Redford reminds me of Hemingway in many ways, a man unsettled somewhere deep down, a man who excels in athletic endeavors and his art with fervor and relentlessness. He's the Hemingway of the late twentieth century, I think, a man whose landscape serves as an outward expression of his inner life. The openness of the West and its inherent lost frontier lend themselves to longing, and in many ways, those of us who desire the open spaces are really just looking for a physical manifestation of our psyches. We are confined within ourselves, and thus we seek a geography that will free us.

In the *Life* article, Redford is referred to as an "unfree spirit." And though for some it may be difficult to imagine the Golden Boy, the Sundance Kid, the grinning Hubbell Gardner of *The Way We Were,* shackled by something like sadness, I think Redford, like others who are sad, must have had a moment in his life when something eluded him, and it created a distance that he could never ignore. When I see his films, I see the space in between. I see a landscape that is lost, a time left behind. I understand being lost, as if there's no place for me, and the wide expanse of a landscape or a highway affords me the opportunity to ignore that, as if unmarked, unknown territory is less threatening.

Hard to think about lost men without thinking of Jack Kerouac. Kerouac knew sadness. He had to; he always wanted to be somewhere else. Excitement, departure, a manic road, an arrival, and its disillusion made up the cycle of his lonely days. Jack uses the word "sad" more than any other in *On the Road.* When Sal Paradise goes to an opera and hears the tenor sing, "What gloom!" he admits that's how he sees life, too.

But you don't have to get as literary as even Kerouac to face bouts of melancholy within the pages of a book. One night, when I was reading to Indie at bedtime, I was struck suddenly by poignancy, something I had not expected from *Happy New Year, Pooh!,* a story about Pooh and Piglet's misunderstanding of the year's end. When they pull December from the calendar, there are no more months, so they decide to make a poem to say goodbye to them, even though Piglet argues that it's too sad. The remainder of the story is an elegy to each month: March's rains and sleets, September's cool and hazy days, or October's colors.

I found myself wanting to put the book down and sob. For even though Tigger and the rest of the Hundred Acre Woods gang eventually turn Pooh and Piglet around, I was sent reeling for the rest of the evening. I have to be careful what I read.

And lately I've been reading Fitzgerald, though perhaps I shouldn't. I've had enough men who have brought me down, but when I read the first few words of his essay "The Crack-Up"—"Of course all life is a process of breaking down"—I know Fitzgerald could sit in a dark bar with me, along with Redford, Hemingway, Kerouac, and Dylan, way into the night, and we'd all have some Sinatra tune in our heads come the wee hours of the morning, though, as Fitzgerald explains, "in a real dark night of the soul it is always three o'clock in the morning, day after day." So it is.

For Fitzgerald, the space is between the vision of who he was in his twenties, a man whose spirit reflected the boom of the Jazz Age, and who he is at age thirty-nine, a man who has "developed a sad attitude toward sadness, a melancholy attitude toward melancholy, and a tragic attitude toward tragedy." It is as if he gave up, or at least gave in to, the darker shades of his self, as if the fanfare of his youth were as fleeting as the boom, and he lost the struggle and lived a permanent Black Thursday. He wrote about the "ability to hold two opposed ideas in the mind at the same time, and still retain the ability to function."

Fitzgerald once packed his suitcase and went a thousand miles out of his way to figure it all out, and what he discovered was that he had to give in to it—that melancholy, that sadness, the tragedy of the existence he felt he was living at thirty-nine. By that time, he was too much in his head to live out the carelessness of his twenties, or *the* '20s.His big escape turned out to be a reification of his entrapment. Escape, in the form of a long highway or a trip across the border, is not available on a daily basis and is ultimately not permanent, so we have to find other ways to get through the day. We find out what we can bear.

Where do we live but in our own minds? Though for some of us, our mind is a space as desolate and beautiful as a Redford scene. We are tortured by the elusive desire, the unknown territory, the person we can no longer be, the darkness that finds us even in the day. We wander, either physically or within the realms of our selves, and it's never going to settle itself; the distance is never going to lessen, the space between will never grow smaller. It is a part of us, this sadness, and to lose it would mean losing ourselves. We do not live here, nor are we far away. We are somewhere in between.

Substance

13. Wild Girl

One afternoon in fourth grade, I came across an empty beer bottle and picked it up with the intention of tossing it beyond the steel merry-go-round, but my aim fell short and the bottle shattered across the concrete. Scared by the question of what to do, I was rescued by the whistle that ended recess. Freed by the call to go inside, I abandoned the scene of the crime and headed for the blacktop, where other kids from my class were already forming a single-file line. Before I could sneak to my place, Mr. Richardson, a lanky man with a blond mustache, pointed to my leg: "Sweetie, you're bleeding." When I looked, I was surprised to see blood from my right knee trickling down my white kneesock. I hoped it would stop so I could avoid having to tell Mr. Richardson what happened. I was afraid of getting in trouble, worried he would assume I'd heaved the bottle on purpose to see it explode into pieces. But the gash in my knee would not cooperate, nor would Johnny Roan, a short, chubby kid who was more than happy to loudly report I had thrown the bottle.

I was a new student that year, and school had begun only a few weeks before, so the kids were naturally suspicious of me and had no reason to include or protect me. For those first few weeks, I spent recess roaming the playground on my own, thankful for the assigned seating during class and afraid to even look up from my Little Debbie in the cafeteria during lunch. The truth was, I'd thrown the bottle to prevent other kids from tripping over it, and beyond that, my father had instilled in me a loathing for anything related to booze, or hooch, as he liked to call it.

Standing there in front of Mr. Richardson, I opted for silence instead of explanation; and after he carefully removed a shard of glass from my knee and applied a Band-Aid, he insisted that I get the broom and pan from his office and go back to the scene of the crime to clean up while he supervised. The scar from that glass is still visible, a reminder of an embarrassing, profound isolation that I would revisit with equal intensity when I checked myself into rehab some twenty-five years later.

Once, in a convenience store with my father, I asked him if I could have a little box of candy cigarettes. "If you get those," he answered, "you'll grow up to smoke." I was too young to know what a logical fallacy was, and too much an admirer of my dad to not believe everything he said. He had already applied that same logic to Shirley Temples, insisting that ordering them would lead to drinking later on. In restaurants, he'd bark at any hostess who suggested we wait in the bar. His firm *no* signaled his belief that mere proximity to bar stools and beer taps was enough to make me a drinker. Or maybe he was protecting my mother from reminders of her childhood, or avoiding his own desire to order a cold one. Maybe it was all of those reasons. Regardless, bars and booze became taunting mysteries I couldn't wait to discover.

So in eighth grade, when Kim Miller stole a beer for me from the crisper where her father kept his stash, I drank it the next morning in my closet. I poured the bubbly, warm beer into a glass and forced it down. I have always been a bit too distracted by the forbidden, so I didn't need a reason or a dare to drink that beer. I just wanted to see what would happen to me if I did. I got a buzz that lasted through Mrs. Wolland's first-period English class.

In high school, I made friends with the kids who had driver's licenses, because they were the ones making beer runs to stores outside city limits on Saturday afternoons. In ninth grade, I rode in the back of Chris Thomas's red Camaro with Stella Lopez and Todd Simpson out to Dolphin Road for a case of beer. I only drank one before Chris dropped me off in front of my house, but that's all it took to plant the first seeds of addiction to the thrilling car ride that promises intoxication.

That same year, Kelly Boyd picked me up in her white Mustang so that we could drive around town, sharing a bottle of Boone's Farm Strawberry Hill. From the passenger seat, I took more than my share of turns while listening to Kelly brag about the size of her boyfriend's penis. I wasn't sure I was ready for penises yet, but Boone's Farm I had no problem with. I spilled a little on my white sweater and was convinced my mother would know it was booze; I was not yet versed in the art of denials and falsifications that can explain smells and stains away. I learned quickly, though, spending the next few years hiding wine coolers in the secret compartment of my car or spending the night with a friend so that I could stay out past my own restrictive curfew.

I quickly discovered that liquor drinks did two things: They got me drunk faster, which I liked, and they didn't taste as bad as beer. In fact, I would prefer liquor until I moved to a town with a beer-only bar in my mid-twenties. The bar was the Wormy Dog Saloon, which was body to body on Ladies' Night, when I'd pay $5 to drink all the beer I could handle until closing time. But during high school, it was Purple Passion or Bartles & Jaymes Wild Berry wine coolers or, on particularly daring nights, Mad Dog 20/20. "Nothing good ever happens after midnight," my father always reminded me when I asked for a later curfew. *Nothing good happens* until *midnight,* I thought. My rhetorical skills were about as weak as my father's logic, but friends were willing to help, covering for me or corroborating events; even some parents admitted they thought my mom and dad harsh beyond necessity.

One night, Gil Gregory carried me to his truck from a concert after buying me so many drinks I couldn't walk. Then he unzipped my pants and stuck his penis inside me in the parking lot of our school. He had to do something to sober me up. That's what he said, anyway. I didn't want to call it rape; at sixteen, my fascination with Gil obscured any indication that he had done something wrong. What happened to me at a party a few years later, however, when a group of guys concocted a strategy to see how drunk they could get me during a game of Mexican, was different. I knew that was rape. And while I don't remember how to play Mexican, I do remember Dusty Granger hitting me when I tried to get away. Days after that party, rumors abounded that I couldn't stop screaming in that bedroom because I was high on cocaine.

A couple of years after that party, I confronted one of the boys, whom I'd remained friends with, and asked him why he didn't do anything. "We all thought you were enjoying it," he said, refusing to discuss it further. That was the last time I spoke to him. Assumptions about my behavior at parties were never flattering, but I alone had created my reputation for being out of control. I had proven many times I didn't know how to behave, and when I'd push the limits, I would often end up standing alone, outside them. During a fight with my father during my last year at home, he yelled that I would go wild once I left home. "Wild! You're going to go wild!" he yelled, as he flailed his arms in some kind of visual affectation of my potential. How far I had come in knowing how to elude my parents. I didn't need to leave home to go wild—I had already gone. And for the next twenty years or so, I would keep going. And I wouldn't stop until I finally gave up and checked myself into a rehab center outside of Salt Lake City, Utah.

14. What I Remember

Thursday nights: I pick my daughter up from school and we go to a little café downtown to hear Jack, the man who manages the liquor store, singing old country music while we eat dinner. It's our one night out of the week. She eats corn dogs, I drink two glasses of chardonnay.

I get tired of not remembering the endings of films I rent, so I start renting films I know can't possibly have an ending that will make any kind of difference, or be any kind of surprise. I tell everyone that Indie is going through a teen film, Lindsay Lohan phase. I can watch *Mean Girls* every night, my little girl invested enough in the plots to not disturb me too much, and I always know the ending, no matter at what point my mind surrenders.

There was a time when I told myself I'd never take Indie into a liquor store. But by that last December we lived in Utah, every employee at the liquor store had given her either a gift or a nickname, Monkey. One even gave her a dollhouse. She created tea parties out of Jack Daniel's shot glasses and acted out puppet shows with those purple velvet Crown Royal bags.

I'm sitting in my eight thirty-five class while my students discuss the reading in small groups. I'm staring at the clock on the wall, counting the hours until I can get home and start drinking.

At some point, I stop putting Indie to bed. No stories, no songs, no lights out. When she starts wanting attention, it takes me away from drinking, so I dope her up with a children's Benadryl tablet or two so she'll fall asleep within the hour. While I notice that my wine consumption is increasing to two big bottles (magnums) instead of one, I fail to notice at first how Indie herself is building a tolerance for over-the-counter sleep aids—until one day I realize that she's up to three tablets without blinking an eye.

I stop paying bills because I'm spending at least ten to twelve bucks per night on wine. Bills are things I consider when the cable gets turned off or the electricity company leaves a shutoff notice on the front door.

Thursday nights with Jack at the café turn into more nights in other restaurants, the two glasses of wine a warm-up to the wine that waits for me at home. If we go out to dinner, I can start drinking earlier, usually around four forty-five. And on nights when I fear that I don't have enough wine at home to get me as drunk as I need to be, going out to dinner is a necessity.

At night Indie creates elaborate games, generally

involving storefronts, in the living room. One night, when she asks me to drive through her restaurant, I tell her, "I'd rather drink."

Serious drinkers are smart. They have to be.

My morning routine consists of finding my cell phone and checking the dialed-numbers log to see whom I called and when. More than once, I wince to see Kenny's number, with a call time sometime after midnight. Yet I feel worse about the messages from friends on my voice mail, returning messages I don't remember leaving, or about pretending to recall a conversation with a colleague I've had the night before on the phone. Most of my part of the conversation sounds something like, "Tell me again . . . " or, "Remind me about . . . ." Through these conversations, I find out that most people are excited to tell their stories again. I'm not even able to remember any of mine.

Blackout drunk: A drinker who forgets everything that happens after a certain point, but who is still able to function. I suspect that my blackout glass is second bottle, first glass. I think.

In the middle of one night just days before rehab: My sitter finds me in the kitchen, looking for something sharp. I pretend the next morning not to remember. I knew exactly what I was doing.

When I scream, "I've had it!" at Indie, she's too young to know it has nothing to do with her. Even though I stand over her and shout it into her little face.

I decide to set some limits, so I choose 7:00 PM as the hour when I can begin drinking. I stand in the kitchen, staring at the clock on the oven. Six fifty-eight. I wait for two minutes to pass and open the fridge.

I keep a duffel bag in my back seat with a bottle of wine in it. A blue Nalgene bottle is my facade. No one will suspect a woman driving down the road and sipping a fine chardonnay from a sports bottle.

The computer on my office desk hides a space next to the wall. In there I keep a plastic cup of wine. One day I'm particularly brazen and put it right in front of me while I talk to a student. From there, I'm sure it looks like water.

In a moment of desperation, I shatter a glass of wine against the side of my new house during the first month I live there. For the next three years, I pick up shards from the grass.

Friends come to my house in the middle of the night to check on me. "What are you doing here?" I ask. "You called" is always their answer. I give up. I give in. I let them sit with me until it all subsides into sleep.

I no longer have hangovers. I do not know what it feels like to be without one.

Indie finds a glass of chardonnay on the end table one Saturday morning and offers it to me. I tell her I don't drink wine in the mornings. A couple of Saturdays later, I concede.

Weekends are a free-for-all because I have nowhere to be, no classes to teach the next day. Football games become the reason for drinking, and the first game usually begins around 10:30 AM.

Jack moves to a different restaurant across from the liquor store on Main Street. We go for a few weeks, but their wine glasses are smaller, and they're not fast enough at getting my second glass. And finally, we just stop going. Instead, I go to the liquor store every day, unless I've just been paid, and then I stock up for a few days, spending $35 to $40 that doesn't last me as long as I think it will. If it's in the house, I drink it.

A friend comes over, notices that I have started a collection of empty wine bottles, with my favorite, Big House Red, lined up along the mantel in my living room. There are at least ten bottles. "How long has it taken you to collect these?" she asks, expecting a longer period than three days. I take them down after she leaves.

I usually remember my evening at some point during the day, like a dream. One day I'm driving down the highway and take an exit, see it as the same exit I took the night before with Indie in the back seat, because she wanted to drive around until she fell asleep.

15. Disappearing

Drinking was always a part of Kenny's and my relationship. From the house where we met and lived together in Minturn, Colorado, where we'd stay up late drinking Shiner Bock on the porch, to the night I drove to Colorado to tell him that I would move back to be with him, to the sidewalk where I screamed at him after a dinner party because the liquor store was closed and I couldn't get any more wine. He often said that my drinking scared him, but I never paid his concern much attention. After all, he drank right along with me. I think he was more scared of the things I said after I'd been drinking, things I shouldn't have said, about the men who would come back strong in my mind after a few too many. But most of the nights were good ones, when we'd drink a few beers and listen to the Marshall Tucker Band, talk about the novel I was teaching, the men at his work. At some point in the evening, Kenny would put down the bottle, and most nights, I would join him for bed. But often I'd find myself crawling over his large frame after he had fallen asleep, going into the kitchen to continue the night on my own.

To my knowledge, he never knew about the hours I stayed up while he snored in the other room, when I'd pull the cork out of a second bottle of wine and sit up on the couch, listening to music I shouldn't have been listening to after so much wine, listening to my thoughts telling me I wasn't living the life I wanted, even though I desperately needed it. I don't know how long I stayed up drinking and feeling far away those nights, but I'd wake in time to destroy all the evidence—pour out the remnants of red wine, stuff the bottles deep in the trash, place the CDs back in their cases, into their slots on the shelf. I never felt guilty about those nights, believing that all I was hiding from Kenny was my distance. Taking some time for myself. Distance, however, cannot be hidden or tucked away in a garbage bag or poured down the drain.

Looking back, I wonder if Kenny intentionally went to bed earlier than he would have some nights, just to escape the hours he knew I was fast approaching after glass number four. Would it have made a difference if he had sat up with me those nights? Probably not. At one point in our relationship, Kenny began working on the road, staying gone for a month or two at a time, which allowed me to find out if I could find on my own whatever it was I wished for on those nights. But when I reenacted my evening-long relationship with wine alone, I knew it wasn't Kenny I was escaping, and my drinking increased at a rapid rate. I found myself digging coins out of the cup holder in my Jeep to pay for a bottle of wine, rotating my liquor store visits so that the men behind the counter wouldn't suspect I had a problem.

One morning, after I had called in sick to school because I was too hungover to go, I called Kenny and confessed, but

only because I couldn't go on. That morning, he was working on the Gulf Coast of Texas, over twenty-four hours away.
"I'm coming home," he said. He drove straight through, telling me he was coming home to help me stop. I gave in, and
when he came home, everything seemed to subside: the distance, my drinking.

Eventually, instead of drinking alone in the dark, I
drank away from home. I started going out with friends,
or meeting friends I knew were already at bars. I'd leave
Kenny at home, drinking with the upstairs neighbors while
they planned their grand construction company. For me, it
was about anyone, any bar; it didn't matter, just as long as
I could get out of the house and remove myself from Kenny.
I can't remember if my nights away were escapes from our
relationship or just clandestine drinking. Probably both.

He didn't stand for it for long. I wouldn't have either.
Yet when we'd talk about it, he'd tell me he couldn't understand why I didn't want to be with him. How can you tell a
person you're hiding something from that what you're doing
is hiding? I'm not sure I even knew what I was doing. I just
know that I'd find the door that led me to a place far away.
Even on nights when Kenny and I sat on bar stools side by
side, I'd turn to the person on the other side of me and start
up a conversation. Sometimes Kenny would join us, but if I
had it my way, I found a way of being in the bar alone, even
when he sat right beside me. Kenny once said that he took
the job on the road to keep us together, that being gone was
his way of staying. When he was gone, I wanted him home.
When he was home, I wanted to be gone, and the only way I

could do that was by drinking. It was a way of settling into myself, somewhere where he could not find me.

One afternoon, I rode my bike to Avogrado's Number, a little bar in town that had a gazebo out back, where I'd go in the afternoons to read and have a few beers. That particular afternoon, I saw Kenny's truck pull up to the bar and wondered about it, because he did his best to leave me to my own spaces. But this time he wanted me to come home, said he'd put my bike in the back of his truck and drive us. Sometimes my distance became exaggerated; this was his way of pulling me back. I remember that I wanted to ride my bike home. I liked the freedom of pedaling down the tree-lined streets, and somehow I saw my bike in the back of his truck as a surrender. Years later, I can see that my decision to take my own trip back to the house was the beginning of our separation, the beginning of our different paths, the streets we would know separately. By the time I walked in the back door of our house, I was in tears, sobbing, about what I didn't know.

The next day I took a pregnancy test. We had already planned a camping trip to Poudre Canyon, a place significant to us for reasons that no one could know but us, but that are probably the same reasons why any space is significant to two people. It was the summer solstice, and we wanted to spend it outdoors, remembering how we had once made love in the rain on the rocks along the Poudre River. We wanted to extend the feeling that emanated from where we had been at the beginning of our love, to celebrate where we were headed, together. But we had been far enough. The test was positive, and instead of using words, I set the stick on the futon next to Kenny and felt life shift.

After a long conversation and a marriage offer that I quickly declined, we decided to keep our date with Poudre Canyon. On the way out of town, I asked Kenny to stop at the liquor store, as usual. Except this time, I had to add, "If I'm going to do this, I need one more beer and one more cigarette." I was willing to go for a sober, smoke-free pregnancy, but I needed to know which beer was to be my last, which drag, which exhale. As we sat around the campfire that night, I popped open a Tecate and fired up a Marlboro Light. Kenny looked on with disapproval.

"Like one more is going to hurt," I said, trying to convince myself and him that a beer in one hand, a cigarette in the other was acceptable accessorizing for the pregnant gal. I stubbed the cigarette out on a log and poured the rest of the beer onto the fire. Kenny surprised me and said that he too would quit: smoking, drinking, even his beloved dipping. It was the least he could do, he said. He was right. But as it would turn out, continuing our relationship beyond that camping trip was like trying to keep a radio station on long after static overcomes it. We had already passed enough miles to know we had to turn the channel. But he pretended not to hear it, and I kept fumbling with the station, sure it would come in clearly once again.

After Indie was born, we struggled for money, so we came up with a $10 deal: If either of us went out, we could spend only ten bucks. In my case, I went out only for an hour or so right after my last class, so I was home every night by six o'clock. It was more than enough for me. Two bucks bought me two beers at a place called The Sink across from the CU campus. After almost a year of no booze, it was plenty to get me back to the buzz I had missed so dearly. But on all those afternoons with my friends, I failed to notice Kenny's burgeoning impatience about my return to regular drinking, especially the part about drinking away from him.

Looking back, I see that my drinking was very limited at that time, and as a new mother, I desperately needed time just to myself. But I often allowed Kenny to guide my perceptions and make me feel guilty about a beer or two after school. So I encouraged him to take more ten-buck times himself—go out with friends after work, go over to one of their houses on a weekend night, develop a life of his own. It was an offer he couldn't refuse, and one I couldn't take back. Our $10 deal eventually dissolved, after I discovered a restaurant receipt showing clear signs of dinner and drinks for two. A bill beyond the $10 limit, and one that I clearly didn't recall. Every night he drove out of our parking lot, he was getting further and further away. One night, when Indie was only three months old, I carried her downstairs and into that parking lot after him, in hopes of getting him to stay home. Sitting in his truck, he could not look at me as he said he was trying to find his life. Dumbfounded, I answered, "I thought we had a life."

I can't remember drinking during those months. I just remember waiting for him to come home. And then waiting turned to begging, and begging turned to being alone. It was after he told me he was leaving that I spent more than ten bucks at happy hour and added a bottle of wine now and again at home. What comforted me more than crying to friends on the phone was diving down into a cheap chardonnay. I remember one good friend knocking on the door one night, pushing a magnum of white wine through the open space in the doorway, and turning to leave. He knew it was all I wanted. I was grateful, couldn't recognize the pattern that was quickly bearing down again. And when Indie and I left for Utah, I took the wine with me.

When we move, we pack up boxes, deciding which to take, which to throw away or give away. Lost in all the promise of geographical distance and a new city, I forgot to deposit the remnants of Kenny's influence on my life into the nearest dumpster. I took him over every mile from Colorado to Utah in my Ford Escape, imagined his blue truck pulling up in front of the new house, even rehearsed what I would say when I opened the door to find him there. His lingering presence was my fault; I moved him there. And when his memory wasn't enough to sustain me, the wine was. I was addicted to the memory of a man and to wine; I couldn't separate the two. Each month that Kenny didn't come back, I drank more.

I remember one night after I had moved in, when neighbors were still asking questions, a woman asked, "Do you think he'll come back and you all can be a family?" I heard her then as hopeful, just as I was, and was thrilled to find a believer. But when I hear her voice now, I hear its inflections: "Do you (honestly) think he'll come back and you all can be a 'family'?" I can hear them only now, because

I couldn't hear anything for too many years. I didn't want to. I didn't want to face anything or admit anything or feel anything. I just wanted to drink.

We don't know how far we can go until we've gone too far. In that corner house in Utah, I went too far. Drinking chardonnay on the porch on nights after I had put Indie to bed descended over a year into waking up in the house, usually on the floor. Not falling asleep, passing out. Lights and TV on. Candles flickering on the end table, or hours past already burned out. Sometimes this happened at 4:00 AM, when I'd wake and focus my eyes, realize I had "dozed off," take a sip from the glass balanced precariously in my hand, then turn out the lights and collapse on top of my bed.

Mornings, just like those long-ago mornings in Colorado, were about finding out what had happened the night before. I'd fumble around, walk into a living room that looked like a crime scene, only it was my crime scene and I had no clues. In search of my smokes, I'd open the front door to the porch, where more than once I found two empty wine bottles, a crumpled pack of Marlboro Lights, and an ashtray that seemed to measure the mystery of the night before with its load. *Fuuuuck.* I'd grab the bottles and the ashtray, still pretending after all that time that I could neatly put away the night, but this time I was hiding the night from myself, even though I had no idea what it had been about. But that wasn't the worst of it. Not even close.

When someone leaves, they're gone. Once Kenny was gone, his part was over. Mine had just begun. I was supposed to reach the coda to his decision: *Let him leave.* I never even looked for it, convinced myself I wouldn't need to play those chords. Kenny's decision, from what I know, took about two months. Getting over him took me three years, and I drank myself through it.

16. Home

My daughter and I moved to southern Utah one week after the final custody hearing in Colorado. In January, at the preliminary hearing, the judge had given me until June twenty-third: "Miss Talbot, you have until June twenty-third to figure out your life." I thought it was a daunting, unfair request, given that I was not the one who had left. It was also an unstable promise, for the judge had the authority to block any move I made away from Colorado, in order to keep Kenny and me close in the best interest of our daughter. It's tough to wait around to find out if someone's going to stop you from going—especially when that someone is a person you love and who is already gone.

If the judge chose to use her authority, she would seriously limit my chances of landing a job in academia. It's tough to explain to a judge that the English field is flooded; that you don't necessarily choose where you get a tenure-track job; that you're still in shock that the maintenance man you fell in love with four years ago has abandoned you, and you're not really sure you can even look across the table at him, let alone convince a university that you're worthy of a job. But by June twenty-third, I had indeed "figured out my life," at least the part of life that had to do with where

I was going to live and where I was going to teach, and that was as far as I could go into thinking about my life, because the rest of it seemed intangible. My good friend once said, "I am not ready to ask myself those questions." And I wasn't. I felt like life was some kind of carnival that had just left town, and stars that might have shone above its empty, littered field were as lost and lonely as I.

I had never really seen stars until I moved to Colorado. I grew up in a state that bragged about its stars, even though the light in the distance from my front yard turned out to be the skyline of Dallas. Nights in Colorado look exactly the way they should look, the way I saw them in the planetarium as a little girl, when they shined above me, magical and abundant. When I was eight, I walked away from the reclining seats and curved ceilings of the planetarium and went home to wait for the sun to set, so that I could find the Big Dipper and Cassiopeia, maybe even Mars, above my own back yard. I had just discovered that there were other worlds, a whole universe. And instead of feeling small in the face of such vastness, I somehow felt powerful, majestic even, to be a part of such intricate and endless design.

So I went home and waited, staring at the night sky in confusion, wondering where the stars had gone, suspecting that the planetarium was just someone's idea of how the sky might be, or just someone else's sky. So I stopped looking at the night sky, figuring I'd never see stars the way I'd seen them that day in the planetarium. But the night I stood under the black, glittery sky of Colorado, I remembered the way I had felt in elementary school, with that overwhelming sensation of marvel at things I couldn't get close enough to.

I met Kenny the summer I moved to the Rockies, when we shared a house with three other people. A summer of waiting tables for me, a summer of wiring fancy mansions in the mountains for him. It was, and still is, the best summer I ever had. "No summer ever came back, and no two summers ever were alike"—a favorite line of mine from Nathaniel Hawthorne. Every night when I got home from work, Kenny and I stayed up late on the back porch after everyone else had long been asleep, and we talked over a few beers, a few cigarettes, trying not to touch each other. When I think about that porch, I see the stars, the moon on the night we stood on the banks of the Eagle River and I watched him while he was not looking, the way I would for years.

Before that summer, I had not known that people like Kenny existed, and once I knew, I felt that I had been wasting my time with other men. Kenny loved life. I had never seen anyone live so intensely. He brushed up and backed up against a lot of dangerous edges, and he left people behind in the process, but I had no way of knowing that at the time. I felt good when he was around, and I wanted to be a part of whatever it was he was doing, whatever he might do next, and that was anybody's guess. I was swayed by what I would inevitably discover to be his irresponsibility, mistaking it then for a freedom I had never known.

A few months after I leaned over to kiss him at the Half Moon Saloon, I left him waving from a gravel driveway to go teach in Texas. I could not wait tables forever; I had just earned my PhD in American literature and felt obligated to use it. Driving away from him, I headed toward Leadville into the tight curves of the mountain highway, and it took a long time to come down off that road, to take a deep breath instead of holding it. I stayed on that road for far too long, but during the eleven-hour drive through southern Colorado, New Mexico, Ratan Pass, and the Texas panhandle, I never once turned on the radio or played a tape. I listened instead to a summer, replaying my first months with the man who would eventually hold my hand through thirty-three hours of labor, only to let it go for good three months later.

Years later, I found myself in an empty house in Utah, where I had accepted my first tenure-track job, a job I had to get permission from the judge to accept. On the first night that Indie and I were there, we slept on the living room floor of a rental house under a ceiling fan that sounded, every once in a while, as if it were going to take off. We had very little in the way of furniture; I had sold most of it to pay for the move. The first time I walked through the spacious house, I didn't see possibility or a new start. I saw a big, empty space. Those rooms looked like all I did not have, every room a challenge, rather than an opportunity. What I really wanted was for Kenny to come to his senses and move to Utah so that we could start our new lives, our new home, together. After being with him all those years, I didn't know how to have a home on my own, how to sleep through the night without rolling him over to stop his snoring, how to sing with the Bread CD without hearing him tell me from the other room to keep singing, how to smoke on the front porch without listening to one of his stories, how to make fajitas without him cleaning the pan.

So I spent most of that first night, and many long nights after, wanting to call him. For so long, I believed it really was that simple, that he was just a phone call away. But he was already living with another woman as I sat solo on my front porch after Indie had gone to bed, staring at the streetlight on the corner of a city he had never seen. It felt strange, scary even, that we both shared spaces the other had never known, would never know. I sat into the early hours of the morning, as the sprinklers came on at the house across the street, drinking wine and not being able to go in and face all the empty rooms of the house. It was not a home to me; it was just the place I was waiting for Kenny to come to.

The summer Kenny and I met, I received a letter offering me a one-year replacement position at the university where I had earned my doctorate. No matter how much I loved being in the mountains and living alongside the Eagle River with Kenny, I had to take the opportunity, convincing both him and myself that I would not get, in his words, too absorbed there. As it turned out, I stayed in Texas teaching literature for only one year. While I loved the classes and the writers, no lines competed with the ones Kenny wrote in his letters. In the end, they were the only two letters he ever wrote, and he confessed they'd taken him three months to write. He'd sent them both at the same time, and in one he compared our love to a slow Sunday drive. That was all it took, and I moved to Colorado and gave myself over to loving him.

Our home was a basement. We lived on Stover Street and the house was blue. I took a job at the local community college, and he worked as an electrician, a job he would keep for only a few months before he was fired for a reason I never found out, even though it meant that I would end up supporting both of us. There were so many signs that Kenny was not the man he promised to be. We seemed to live separate from the rest of the world, convinced, like so many young couples, that no one could know or had ever known the kind of love between us. How magical everything seemed when we were together. Like on the first night we went to bed in that basement and found the stars. Constellations, planets, meteors, the rings of Saturn. He turned off the bedside lamp and a universe neither of us had expected opened above us, a secret sky. An unexpected gift from the person who had lived there before us, or maybe even the person before that, the one who had carefully attached glow-in-the-dark constellations and planetary systems onto the ceiling, so that it seemed as if we were in the middle of nowhere when we lay in bed at night, looking up at a black, starry sky.

We made a home of that small place, living underground with exposed pipes in our living room, the thud of a basketball from one of the boys who lived above us. I remember all of it: the wind chime that hung outside the door, the window smeared with our fingerprints from the night we made love outside against it, the sunlight coming through the kitchen window on mornings we drank chai, the *chimenea* that he bought so that he could build us a fire every night, the green chair we took from someone's sidewalk, the ice on the sidewalk the night we shuffled home from the bar, the three-mile loop to the Colorado State University campus that we ran every other night. I remember the sounds of wood splitting as he cut it into small enough pieces. Jack Kerouac wrote that you could tell a lot about a man by the way he chops wood. On the camping trip we took on the weekend I found out I was pregnant, I took a picture of Kenny doing just that so I could remember that idea, the character of a man existing in the arc of the swing, the give of the wood. Sometimes I get out the picture to see if I can see the leaving in his stance.

At our home in Utah, I had to face the fact that Indie and I had no place to sit in the living room, that I didn't have a bed, that we didn't have a shower curtain, that I didn't have any money until school started and I received my first paycheck. Even then it would be tight, and I couldn't afford to buy more than one item at a time. So each month, I added or good people gave; I even traded in the kitchen table where Kenny and I had sat all those mornings for a new one, but Indie and I still ate all of our meals on the living room floor. To me, dinner at a kitchen table was family time, and I didn't feel like a family. I thought of us as what had been left over from a family, or what had been left behind. All I could think about was how Kenny had complained that the old table had been too narrow for his six-foot-two frame, his large legs, and how it didn't matter anymore. I put the new table together one night in my living room after Indie had gone to bed, and I didn't feel brave or self-reliant turning the screwdriver, tightening the seat backs. I felt hollow, my loneliness an echo no one knew to listen for.

Kenny and I never had much; in fact, on the day Indie was born we had $4 in the bank. We struggled, but we still found hours to read Raymond Carver poems or discuss a Hemingway story he had just read for the first time, and nights on the porch next to the fire, as we took turns running down to the basement to get more beer and change the CD from Bread to Waylon Jennings to the Marshall Tucker Band, with his favorite song that bragged, "I ain't never been with a woman long enough for my boots to get old," a song that proclaimed, "I never had a damn thing, but what I had, I had to leave it behind." I have learned to pay attention to the words of somebody's favorite song, and I keep Kenny's fly rod in a closet; it was his most prized possession. I keep it for Indie, so that she knows where he found the best part of himself, where he was at peace, so that someday when she asks why he did not stay, and the answer of restlessness and wandering cannot be any answer for her when it never seemed to solve any of his problems, at least she can have the part of him that was quiet.

I will also tell her of the nights we, overwhelmed, cried over how much he and I loved. Such abandon, like the night we took turns reading chapters of a book to her as she grew inside me. He held on to me and cried. Maybe we did that because we were afraid. Perhaps we didn't trust our love, felt its tremors beneath the surface, knew that it could not hold.

When Kenny left, I moved into another basement, one in the house of some good friends who gave Indie and me a home when we could not afford one of our own. I was still allowing Kenny to come around then, and I was still sharing my bed, even though we had our impending custody hearing, the one my future would be beholden to on June twenty-third. I ignored court dates and notarized documents in favor of turning it all around, or at least stopping the direction we were headed in. I even stuck stars to the ceiling in some attempt to bring him back, make him remember. When you love someone after they've stopped, you work to re-create any memory, any moment, as if you can nudge a person back to an emotion. And that is where we fail, because we are not the sun to the planets of emotion. Quite the opposite. They come and go as they please, a separate universe. Some of them never return, no matter how much they are summoned, and we wait much longer than we should for one to reappear, like a comet. And still there are those that take longer to fade than we can stand. But for months I believed that if I turned the ceiling of an unfamiliar basement into a starry sky, he would remember, and he would come back.

But it didn't turn out that way; I remember he even laughed. I pulled the stars down the next morning, realizing that I was trying to get him to come back to nowhere, because he'd come to visit me in a place where I felt forced to be, because he'd left us, and left me feeling as if I had nowhere to go. I felt betrayed, saw myself and those little stars as silly. Those plastic things had nothing to do with bodies moving together, or laughter in the dark. They had to do with loss, with sleeping in the middle of the bed.

I still can't sleep in the middle of the bed, and some nights that's because Indie flails and lands with her feet in my neck. But most nights, it's because I just can't. For months after Indie and I had been in our new city, I dreamed that Kenny was standing just outside the house. He would be in the yard, on the sidewalk, trying to get in, but he never did, or I would never let him. Such obvious fear, for I had been working hard to make this space my own, mine and Indie's; he had no place here, and for the first time I was afraid instead of hopeful that he would come back. I worried that he might tear down all I had built on my own—all that Indie and I had built together—and he had already taken so much.

Just a few weeks after we took Indie home from the hospital, I spent my nights standing at the window, waiting to see Kenny's blue truck pull into the drive, never wanting to believe that he would come home only when he had to. He distanced himself from Indie and me. He wouldn't even go in to kiss her goodbye when he left for work, or put her to bed when I was exhausted from school and asked for help. "I don't want to get too attached," he mumbled. But instead of hearing the truth, I tried harder to make it as easy as possible for him to stay, by doing the laundry; letting him sit in front of his junkyard show without ever interrupting; setting his food on the coffee table without so much as a "here you go," for fear that too much of my presence might erupt into his leaving; buying groceries and making several trips up and down the steps just weeks after a cesarean. Looking back, I realize he was working to get me to kick him out, so that it would never be that he had left, but that I had asked him to leave.

On the night when I finally gave him permission, he packed up and carried things down the stairs to his truck: my guitar, my CD player, a few pots, his coffee mug, my belief that I could count on anything, my faith that shared memories, a child, could be enough to sustain someone's heart. And even though we will never be together again, even though he never calls, never comes to see his daughter, I realize that I will always have those memories, this girl. I have just as many memories with her, and every day she does something else that only I get to see, like when she reaches over in the middle of the night and says, "Mom" and hugs me in her sleep.

One year after Indie and I moved to Utah, we no longer had a house or a place where I waited; we had a home, and all of the rooms were full and warm, and candles burned every night, offering not shadows, but assuredness. Indie never did sleep in her own bed, but I didn't mind; most of the time she made me feel better than I did her to wake in the middle of the night and find her there. But I worked to redesign her room that summer anyway, to give her a place that was special and her own. A room she showed everyone who came to the house, a room she called "beautiful." I draped tulle over her bed, put up twinkle lights around her windows, and, for the final touch, I decided to add one more thing: stars. I loved the way something simple could be majestic, that I took small plastic stars, put some adhesive on them, and gave my daughter her own sky.

On the afternoon when I stood on a blue chair in the middle of her room, sticking the stars to her ceiling, it hit me. I had not even thought of the connection as I rushed to the store for the final piece of her new room. With stars in my hands and above my head, I remembered that she had been made under a ceiling of stars. It seemed only right that she now have her own sky, one that Kenny will never see. For a moment, I felt sorry for him that he would not know of this starry sky in our lives. But then, for the first time, I felt lucky. I had found something I had never seen, a universe rich with history, with love, with feelings I thought had eluded me forever. I had come very far to be here and it made sense, these stars in her room, her life, her dreams.

I spent the first two and a half years of Indie's life looking back at an old one, leaving my heart behind and wondering where life might be found again, where love might
be trusted. And while I will complain about any novel that
ends with a woman who searches for herself only to find a
man, here I had been doing just that. Telling myself that I
had been but was no longer. I must have seemed a ghost to
my daughter, moving through rooms and looking out windows, seeing branches spread across the snow and crying
because they reminded me of reaching for nothing.

And all that time, this person was beside me, growing
from infant into little girl, into a person who loves to run, to
sing with her arms spread wide, to pat me on the back when
I'm down, to give people what they seem to need without
asking, the same way her father read people so well and listened. This little girl who is bright and good, who loves life
with the same intensity as her father; the one kids wait for
at school, crowding around her and shouting her name with
glee when she walks in the door, reminding me of the way
no evening seemed to start for anyone until Kenny arrived.
Indie has so much of the good in him, and so while I knew I
had to let him go, I also had to embrace the beauty she came
from, the gifts we both gave her.

I had always seen the love Kenny and I shared and the
love Indie and I share as separate worlds, but now I know
that those loves exist on a continuum of constellations. All
the time I had been waiting for him to come back, for stars
to shine again, I had been waiting for the wrong thing. Everything came after all; everything came through her.

17. Wild Bill's Words

I feel fortunate to write Bill's story. "Fortunate," a feeling word. Bill would say "blessed." But Bill is his own story. I'm just writing it. In rehab, when we went around the circle before meditation every morning at seven fifteen, Bill didn't join the rest of us who had dragged in to collapse on mats in the gym. Bill was large, even claimed to gain twenty pounds during his stint in the Ridge, eating a trayful at each meal, to the point that sitting or lying down became uncomfortable for him. It was also dangerous for us. Once, during rec, Bill leaned over to stretch and cleared the gym in five minutes with his gas. We didn't allow him to stretch after that; we forced him to lean against the far wall of the gym while we warmed up for volleyball. He'd sit in exile, laughing, grinning in his long-sleeved black button-down and jeans.

But even when Bill wasn't in the middle of things, we could feel his presence. He was a spiritual leader with more faith in God, his Higher Power, than any of us. Or at least he said he did. He had to, I imagine. Some of us needed to believe more than others—and not because of the booze or the drugs. Some of us had been so mistreated or forgotten that we'd never had a reason to believe in anything or anyone, especially ourselves and our ability to control our own lives. I'm not questioning Bill's sincerity; I'm just saying he needed it, and he needed the rest of us to believe. It was like he was trying to save us all with his god, because he had learned years ago that he couldn't save anybody on his own. He had a wife at home who was quickly learning how to save herself, too. But every time it was Bill's turn to introduce himself, it was the same: "I'm Wild Bill, alcoholic, addict. And I feel very blessed today."

Bill had health problems. High blood pressure, depression. He was on meds, like the rest of us, and he was allowed to keep a small water bottle with him during meetings. One of the rules prohibited us from bringing food or drink to the meetings. I'm not sure why. Just another rule for us to follow. None of us knew how to follow rules, and we surely hadn't followed them in our own lives. That's why we were there. We made up our own. Bob Dylan said that if you were going to live outside the law you had to be honest. We weren't that, either. At one point or another, we all challenged the rules, assuming they shouldn't apply to us. But Bill's high blood pressure meds made him cough, and the fits would get so bad, he'd sometimes have to leave the room. That wasn't allowed during meetings, either—not coughing, not leaving. That rule had to do with respect. Another thing we needed to learn, because we didn't have respect for anything, most of all ourselves.

On the nights when our meetings didn't end too late, we'd meet in the big room and watch a rented movie. Another rule: No R-rated movies, no movies with excessive sex, booze, or drugs. Violence seemed to be acceptable, as the men of the group watched *Troy* two or three times during the week it was rented. A few of the more strong-minded women eventually insisted on having more of a say in the movie selections, but none of us were willing to indulge in romance or overly dramatic films, and since it was Christmastime, we usually opted for films like *Elf* or *Scrooged*. We'd move the chairs away from the walls and place them together in front of the television, bring blankets and pillows, and pretend that we were cozied up in our own homes. One night a man named Andy said, "I just want to hold your hand for a minute. That all right?" And it was.

Someone would add to the domestic illusion by coming in and out of the laundry room every twenty minutes or so, folding shirts and underwear, putting someone else's load into the dryer, always apologizing for handling intimates. None of us minded. We'd all exposed ourselves way beyond boxers and bras. I scooped up Bill's laundry once and dropped it all, jeans heavy with their size and gray underwear, into the dryer. Bill always joined us for the movies, so we had to turn the sound up enough so that he could hear, and even louder during his throat-clearing episodes.

"I'm deaf, so please speak up!" he would yell. We heard it a hundred times a day; at the opening of every meeting, when he shared his stories or steps, when he spoke at the local AA, Bill told the same stories again and again. Someone once said that if Bill needed to tell the train story again or the meth story one more time, it was part of his recovery. So we all stopped looking at the floor with impatience or embarrassment and watched Bill, listened to see if the story would change. It never did. For a man who was "nearly illiterate," Bill's booming voice related his story each time with the same words and inflections. Maybe he didn't know how to change the narrative, maybe he didn't know how to rearrange the events.

Some stories Bill had in his head would never change. One story he had never told. When his counselor told him to write it, he did. Then he read it in group and never mentioned it again, except when he allowed me to read it one night after I said I would like to. But those other stories, the train one, the meth one, Bill needed to hear again, even though we all had before and before that, too. Bill must have wanted to remind himself that he had been close to killing himself, killing someone else. Because this was Bill's second time around, and he hadn't learned the first time. He had thirteen years of sobriety on the day he climbed into some guy's truck outside the Lowe's in Portland. He hadn't had a drink in three months, but booze wasn't his drug of choice. Meth was a different story. Bill liked to tell it.

Bill had dark hair and a thick beard heavy with gray. When he got hot, which he often did because of the meds or his belly, he'd take off his glasses and wipe the sweat from his eyes. He called the men "bud," the women "sweetie." It was clear that Bill had worked around men most of his life. He was gruff, sometimes crass, once complaining that he had to flush the toilet two or three times to "get it all to go down." Though he went by the moniker "Wild Bill," what I saw and came to know of him was more gentle than wild. Bill's good nights to me, as I stepped between the chairs on

my way to bed on movie nights or shuffled down the hallway in my PJs and black slippers at lights out, were comforting: "Good night, sweetie." Usually, I'd scoff at being
labeled as "sweetie" or "hon," but here I let it go. Bill and I
came from different worlds. He meant it. I could hear that.
His good morning greetings were equally comforting.

Bill met his wife on the first of May 1971 and married her
exactly a year later. She was agoraphobic, and he had never
been away from her. He worried about her back home in
Portland, worried that she wouldn't use the number of the
neighbors he had left her if she needed groceries. He talked
to her on the phone every night, encouraged her to walk
out of the house far enough to check the mail. But as we
learned, through each story we told or listened to, recovery
wasn't just limited to those of us locked in the Ridge. Being
in rehab gave everyone a space for healing, those we had
hurt, ignored, abandoned, everyone we had wronged.

One day, not long before Bill "coined out," a ceremony
on the day you leave rehab where you are presented with a
thirty-day coin, his wife called to tell him that she'd called
the neighbors, told them she needed bread. When he shared
that in group, we all clapped, and it wasn't an automatic,
"glad you're finished talking" clap. We were sincere. The
thing about rehab is that you grow to love or loathe the
people you hear about. We all worried about Bill's wife and
wanted so much for her to get that mail, but she went even
further. Bill's wife got the bread. Without Bill. It was a first.

I heard a few weeks after I left that when Bill got home, she told him that she had discovered something while he was gone: She could make it without him, so he'd better behave. Before he had gone to rehab, she had given him the ultimatum that all of us had heard in one form or another: *Do it again and I'll leave.* But her threat, as he knew, was empty. How could a woman afraid of stepping out onto her own sidewalk step away from her husband? But now her warning carried all the weight of the train car Bill had backed into a coworker.

Bill's at the Lowe's hardware store when he runs into an old buddy.

"Man, have you tried this new shit they have on the street?"

Bill says no. He's been sober for thirteen years.

The story skips ahead to the parking lot.

Bill remembers, "When I took that first line, it nearly blew my face off. I took three more."

Bill goes to work the next day. He's a foreman. He told me once on the smoking porch that while he couldn't read or write, his boss didn't care, said he had other skills, said Bill knew how to lead his men, how to take care of them.

"I had the thing in reverse, going about eight miles an hour, when I heard a man scream and I knew I had done something bad." Bill shook his head at this point in the story. Every time.

Bill hops down from the train and sees his coworker crumpled on the ground, holding his arm. When he gets closer, he sees that the man is bleeding from his right eye.

While they wait for help, the man looks up at Bill and asks if he can pray. "God, please help something positive come out of this situation."

Bill had broken the man's arm. After Bill told the story, he would claim that the man's prayer had brought him to rehab. The man wasn't mad, but they tested Bill for drugs and the meth showed up. Railroad policy: Go to rehab or get fired. His wife had been telling Bill that God needed to slap him upside the head. The man's prayer and his wife's wish had come true. He felt that he was given a second chance, and this time, he'd say, "I'm going to do it His way, not my way. My way didn't work."

I never said this to Bill, but I think it was more than his willingness to let his god work in his life. I think it was the story he wouldn't tell that had such a grip on him.

I loved to hear Bill laugh. He put the whole weight of his body behind it, and when we were out smoking, a new habit his wife didn't know about, he'd laugh at himself more than anything else, which always made me laugh. Once, he came out to the porch with his discharge form and asked me to write his history for him. I told him to tell me what to write, and I'd write just that. I knew the details already, but I let him say them once again, as I sat out in the cold of a late December afternoon at the table and Bill sat across from me, leaning over to tell me his history: "Began using alcohol at the age of fifteen. Pot usage. Meth. Went to AA but stopped going to meetings. Thirteen years of sobriety. Relapse. Three months without alcohol. Came to the Ridge." I wanted to add: "He told the story. He remembered those men." But it was not my history. I wrote Bill's words as he spoke them.

He trusted me with his words, to record them, spell them, read them. He'd ask me every time I sat next to him in the cafeteria if I was going to write about "this place," as he called it. I assured him I would, watching him smile and yell to another table, "She's going to write about us!" Most of them had asked, at one time or another, if I would write their story. It seemed important to them to be given a voice, a voice they couldn't give themselves, but for Bill, it went beyond that. He was fascinated by, and admired, my ability to write, my status as a professor. Maybe it was because he could barely read, each word a mountainous obstacle, and when he wrote, the difficulty nearly strangled him, so he stuck to only a few words, ones he knew, like "His way" and "Portland yards."

Big Book Study was once a week, and we all had to take turns reading a paragraph from a chapter. When Bill's turn came to read at any meeting, the person sitting next to him would prompt when Bill stopped in silence, confusion, pretending that his glasses were the cause. It was one of the most beautiful offerings I remember seeing in that place, how everyone would help Bill read, as if he were the slow kid in elementary school and his best friend wanted to keep his secret, so he'd whisper the right words into his ear. One night at closing, when Bill shared his low for the day, he said, "That Big Book Study," and we all looked down, wanting to give Bill the ability to read the words or the ability to understand that he was safe, even in his falterings over words the rest of us knew. We all had shortcomings, but most of them we could hide. Not this one, as reading and writing were integral to recovery at the Ridge.

Someone long ago, in school or in childhood, had let Bill down. And here, when he was already stripped of all control and power and authority, his inability to join the rest of us in a simple reading leveled him. But just as we were all discovering what we couldn't do and surprising ourselves with what we could, the next day Bill came in to rec, not with his long-sleeved black shirt, and not straight to his self-relegated position of spectator along the wall, but onto the court with a teal tank top and a black brace on his left elbow. Bill was best at the center position, tall enough to defend half of his side of the court. The next day, when Bill came to rec in his black again, I yelled across the gym to ask if he was going to play. His face lit up, and he turned around and briskly left the gym. In a few minutes, the tank top re-emerged and Bill took his position on the court, laughing, clapping his large hands together and shaking his head at the ground between each volley. On those days I didn't mind if I had to rotate out during a game. I just liked watching him play.

As large as Bill was in his frame, he was frail in health and, in some ways, still a boy. A nineteen-year-old boy who had gone far away from home, away from the father he could not satisfy. The youngest brother of three who didn't love football like his father's other sons. He signed up for the Army, believing that what he had at home didn't leave any space for him to prove himself. He spent six months in Vietnam. He saw three of his friends die.

Jack, a counselor at the Ridge, was a tough son of a bitch. For Jack, it wasn't, "I'm an alcoholic" or, "I'm an addict" after his name when he led group, it was, "I'm 4A." When a newcomer had the courage to ask, because it took courage to speak directly to Jack, he'd list off, starting with the thumb of his only hand: addict, alcoholic, amputee, asshole. He was a short, stout man who tucked the left sleeve into the armhole of his polo shirts, making the large, color tattoo on his right forearm more prominent. He was Bill's counselor, as he was to most of the railroaders. I suspected it was about the toughness of those men, the reticence that Jack wouldn't put up with, the sick shit Jack had done that made him the right man for those men who prided themselves on being men. He certainly was the right man for Bill.

Bill told me that God had brought them together, said he could talk to Jack, that they could talk to each other. It was more than a counselor/patient relationship with those two; it was two broken men who had nightmares. About war. About the whistle of gunfire from ghosts. About the faces of friends blown off. About signing over your arm even though you were underage. I never heard Bill's autobiography, the one in which he mentioned those three boys, because he was in another group during step session, but he let me read about them. It was an assignment. Jack said it was more about honoring the men than anything else, but I suspect it was about Bill saying goodbye. Either way, it was an assignment, and Bill felt comfortable with such demands from a fellow soldier.

One night I noticed Bill pacing around the lounge, catching my eye now and again. I got up, knew he wanted to show me something. "I got those things I wrote about those boys," he offered, in a less sure and sound voice than usual, "if you want to read them." I did. I followed him. We found some chairs away from everyone, and he shuffled through his folder, putting the pages in order. Said it was important to read them that way: one, two, three. I didn't know what to expect, and I didn't know what to say. I waited while he struggled to organize the papers. When he handed them to me, I began to read as Bill leaned back in one of the chairs he'd grabbed from the meeting room, sighing heavily as he often did. He disappeared as I found myself in a war between a man and his memories, felt myself along a river with young boys who were asked to clean up along the river. I never asked Bill to clarify what it meant to clean up, because I was afraid of the answer. What struck me about his duty involved the vulnerability to shots from phantom guns that he and his fellow soldiers never saw. They were open targets.

After I read pages one, two, and three, Bill spoke for a while, until words would not work anymore. He took off his glasses and wiped his eyes, not from the heat, but from tears. I didn't feel worthy to be the recipient of what Bill had shared. I wasn't experiencing only the guilt of a boy who survived; I was feeling my own guilt about knowing that I could never understand anything he had seen. So what could I say? Words wouldn't work for me, either. What Bill saw was still real to him. At one point while he talked, he looked down at his usually folded hands stretched out in disbelief. He was back at that river, and he had taken me with him. Selfishly, I told myself I could walk away from that place, but the weight of an afternoon, a moment, remained heavy, immovable from Bill's lap.

At this point, I want Bill to tell his own story, their stories. He gave pages one, two, and three to me on the day he left the Ridge. I imagine these are the most words Bill will ever write. I feel honored to include them here.

What Was Joe Lovett Like?

Joe Lovett was a yung idao spud. One hell of a grate guy that we called Spud. All he coughted is talk about Betty. He love to smoke pot and drink beer and stair at Bett pitchers. She was a pairty littal thing. He love to cut trees down with this fifty calorber gun. But we all now he didn't get to go home. He was the first of the three to be shot in the head. I will always remember him like a brother. God Bless him. He was bless for "19" of his life.

What Was Mike Stratton Like?

Mike Stratton was big boy. He look lik he cought cut trees down with two chops. But he was one big tedy bear. We all called he Miky. Miky was from Orchers Washington. He was ok until we got him riped. He cought of hurt any one of us when he was riped and in a rage. I got know Miky for only "26" days. He was number two of three to be shot in the head. In the short time I got to know him I loved him like he was my brother. Now I know why we all were num all the time we were there. We all tried to not think about it. Like Spud Miky was bless with "19 years of life. I will never for get them. They will always be in my hart and in my prairs. God Bless Them.

What Was John Bires Like?

John Bires was a nice guy. He wought have given you any thing He was from New York. One of those guy that talk funny. He loved to smoke pot. Then he wought eat every thing. You think he talk funny. When he was riped he talked even funnier. I got know him longer than Spud or Miky. For fun we called him JB. Have you ever hered some one from New York called JB. JB loved to play cards. He won a lot of the time. I hated to play cards with him. He always took my money. I got to know JB longer then Spud or Miky. JB was there for two months. JB was three of three to die. JB also was shot in the head. But this time his head landed in my lap. I just sat there with his head bleeding in my lap. I felt like I wasn't there. I will never forget them. I will have them always in my hart. May God Bless them all my Brother.

18. Park City Queen

Maybe that bottle I threw in fourth grade, sending its shards into my knee, was a bad omen. It's my earliest recollection of a sense of bottomless isolation, a painfully embarrassing moment from childhood that was undoubtedly wrapped up in my father's feelings about alcohol. And yet, etched as that experience is in my memory, it pales in comparison to the memories that haunted the women I met in rehab.

Maddie, my roommate, checked in with a black eye she couldn't remember getting, though she assumed she'd hit it on the edge of a coffee table when she blacked out. Elizabeth had stabbed herself in the chest with a kitchen knife shortly after opening her third bottle of chardonnay; she had called 911 just before losing consciousness. Ellen, a former craps dealer, had shredded her liver to pieces; I watched her shuffle through the hallways, barely able to function at the age of fifty. Tracy had been busted for the meth lab in her basement, and even inside the Ridge, she wore her leather jacket. So many of the women covered themselves in sweatshirts or long-sleeved robes, though not because it was winter. It was something about needing to feel safe, whether through a facade of toughness or the comfort of thick cotton. Only Leslie bared her arms, revealing scars from years of cutting.

There were many women in rehab who had wounds from their childhoods, or their twisted husbands, some visible, others apparent only when you looked into their eyes. Some of them were putting up a good fight to keep their kids or their jobs, to overcome yet another DUI charge, but too many of them were failing at their struggles with the men they had—not one of those bastards worth anything, and many of them a contributing factor to their wife's or girlfriend's addiction. I didn't meet one man in rehab who didn't have a loving, supportive companion back home. I never met a woman who did.

Women develop an addiction to alcohol at a faster rate than men do, and, as one counselor told us, a woman can dissolve into debilitating dependency in as few as thirty days. Most of the women in rehab, like me, began drinking at an early age, another factor that can lead to alcoholism. But it's not the thirty days or the drinking at thirteen that they're interested in when you check yourself into rehab; they want to know the reason you drink. That's what we have to figure out, and the best way to do that is to write an autobiography of our drinking or using lives. We listened to each other's stories, but the one I came to know the best was Maddie's.

Maddie had been in and out of rehab two times already, though her previous stints had been at Betty Ford. I never asked her why she hadn't gone there again, maybe because she didn't remember how she got to the Ridge in the first place. The staff encouraged us to remember how—and why—we got there. "Remember" may not be the correct word, though. Each of us, at one time or another, had to be told what we did or said on the day or night of our arrival, and what transpired during detox. In Maddie's case, she told every person she saw to fuck off, and kept yelling about how this place was a dump, and how much nicer Betty Ford was. Her husband probably dropped her off after finding her passed out on the floor with a black eye while their four-year-old son slept upstairs.

Maddie, like me, was a wino, a woman who didn't limit her pinot grigios and beaujolais to the cocktail parties and soirees of her circle. Add to that a penchant for Xanax. I called her the "Park City Queen" because she lived in an affluent town and expected to be treated like royalty in a place that used plastic sheets on the beds. She was very blond, very thin, very attractive, and very, very bored in her life. On the outside, she fit that ideal beauty standard: highlights, capped teeth, flawless skin, size 0. But in the privacy of the room we shared, Maddie was anything but confident, and spent most of her time asking me what people said or thought about her.

When Maddie read her autobiography during group, she often used the word "perfect" to describe her family. Her counselor attributed much of Maddie's drinking to the impossibility of such attainment, and to Maddie's inability to cope with the inevitable letdown. When I finally met Maddie's husband, I suspected that his closet homosexuality presented another obstacle in her quest for the perfect marriage. She spoke of the tension in their marriage, and I'm sure it made that Xanax go perfectly with a high-dollar chardonnay. Like me, Maddie was a white-wine woman, though she didn't have to limit her selection to price. I can also guarantee that she never had to witness her own priorities come into question by drinking the electricity and the phone off, the way I did. She described the special wine refrigerator she and her husband had in their kitchen, the one he put a lock on to keep her from drinking thousands of dollars a night.

She was a card-carrying member of AA, tacking her Park City phone list and sponsor's number on her side of our bulletin board like flyers announcing her commitment. She quoted the AA blue book, and in group she proffered herself as some veteran who should be awarded medals for her knowledge of the principles of AA. Yet she was an addict. She was an alcoholic. And the fact that she didn't know it, didn't own it, was where she so clearly failed. She spoke the words at every meeting, but she didn't believe them. Instead, she spouted off lines from chapters five or six, never realizing that not one of us wasn't thinking about the fact that she was here for the third time, each of us too cynical to trust her so-called expertise.

One day, after I'd stormed out of a meeting in tears, I expected her to come back to our room ready with sympathy or additions to my scathing evaluations of the program. Instead she told me that she knew how it worked, that she had been through rehab enough to know that the goal was to break us down. "You have to let go. You have to let them help you, and you have to know you can't be in control." She was angry as she relayed her assessment, but looking back, I think she was frustrated that it had taken her three times to figure that out. I told her it was my first time, thank you very much, and I didn't yet have her vast experience to know to just let go, and I wasn't about to let anyone but me have control. "Except the wine," she shot back. I told her to fuck off. I wasn't about to take advice from her. She wasn't exactly credible.

In our room later that night, when we were forced to be in bed by lights out at eleven, she confided that she really enjoyed the social aspect of the AA meetings and the lunches in Park City. And that's what it was to her: some kind of club with high membership fees. Toward the end of her twenty-eight days, she came back from a home visit with a bottle of pills and a cell phone, keeping both hidden in a drawer under some sweaters. I never asked her about them, nor did I ask how she got them past the nurses' station. But once she had those pills, she was a different woman. She was not manic or cripplingly insecure, as she had been during the weeks I had known her. She was a Stepford alcoholic, all smiles and pleasantness that eventually convinced the counselors and staff that it had finally sunk in and Maddie had made a real turnaround. What she had made, I wanted to tell them, was a visit to her pharmacy. At times, I feel guilty for not revealing the source of her newfound disposition, because now I know that on her first night home from rehab, she went straight for the wine. The third stint in rehab would not be her last.

It's difficult to be a writer in rehab. Most of the program is built upon cognitive therapy, an approach that allows the patient to take an active role in her recovery. At the Ridge, most of that cognitive therapy involved writing, and each step had an assignment that we had to complete and present to the group. The group was allowed, and encouraged, to participate by offering feedback. It was a writers' workshop for drunks. According to Maddie, my detox rant went something like this: "I came to rehab to write a fucking essay? I'm pissed!" For most people in the Ridge, writing was excellent therapy. Most of them hadn't written anything beyond a check (and mostly hot ones at that) for decades. Writing gave them a means of contemplating their lives and recording their addictions in a way that forced them to face themselves and their damage. Yet for me, writing was a career, and I had been helping other people write their stories for years. I felt cheated and frustrated. I kept insisting that I had written about most of it already. Why did I have to write it again?

When it came time for me to present Step One, my autobiography, I did just that. I wrote an essay. I even went through drafts, crossing out sections, adding paragraphs, creating a motif, a recurring metaphor, an ending that slid down like melting ice cream on a cone. When I finished reading the eleven pages, front and back, Jeff, a twenty-two-year-old bartender who had passed out with a gun in his hand, thus foiling his suicide plan, spoke first: "Do I have to write like that?" Jeff's comment surprised me, because he had become my book buddy, passing books to me as fast as he could read them: Chuck Palahniuk, David Sedaris, Denis

Johnson, and James Frey's *A Million Little Pieces,* which became a kind of contraband due to its "AA is bullshit" theme. But Jeff and I both liked the conclusion Frey comes to at the end: *Drink or don't drink. It's that simple.*

After Jeff spoke up, the counselor informed everyone that I was an English professor and a writer, but that what we all needed to focus on was what I wrote, not how it was written. Most of the people in the group, in rehab, according to my counselor, had never met someone like me. It was hard for them to get past the writer and get to the wino. Yet I'm not sure my counselor assuaged their anxieties. He asked me, after I finished reading, "If you had to sign your name to that writing, how would you?"

"Jill L. Talbot," I answered.

"Not 'Doctor'?" he pushed, and I didn't understand where he was going.

"No, just the name."

"Do you have any nicknames?"

"My brother and some people who know me well call me Jilly."

"Who is Jilly?"

"Good question."

After that, I was known as Jilly, and I hoped that by hearing her name, I might find her again. I did, and during my final days there, I worried that returning to campus, to my office and my classroom, might make her disappear. One day Leslie enlightened me: "You're Jill and Jilly. You don't have to lose one to be the other." I am still working to remember that.

Many times during group sessions, counselors and psychologists would warn us that some of us weren't being honest, and that unless we got honest, we'd never recover. I'd look around the room, silently chastising those too stubborn to come clean. I'd often implored my students to be honest for the sake of their essays. "Write it or don't" was a refrain in my writing workshops. So I was very surprised to learn, after a couple of weeks of counseling sessions and presenting my steps, that I was not being honest. In my writing. I couldn't shake another refrain from my teaching: "Be more loyal to the art than what created that art." So how was I supposed to learn to invert that in twenty-eight days or sooner, and just write what happened? That wasn't enough. But in rehab, that's what it took. One counselor went so far as to give me an assignment. After reading a three-page essay, he told me to write it as a haiku. That night I sat outside in the hall with my back against the wall after lights out and quickly wrote the following.

> I am tired of me.
> I want to write life, not art.
> I don't like alone.

I had been stripped. I was, for the first time since I had been there, vulnerable. For most others, reading aloud meant vulnerability; for me, however, it was a non-event—something I was accustomed to. And when I shared my writing—even my most personal writing—no one talked to me about their impressions of my story, my life. Instead I heard what a good writer I was. Wild Bill would always say,

"You write so pretty." I heard it too much, in fact. In some ways, I had a twenty-eight-day ego boost, but the fact that no one could get past my words to what I was saying became increasingly problematic.

"You're hiding between those beautiful lines," my counselor admonished. "No one doubts you can write. But can you allow yourself to get out from behind them?" I heard my brother's voice from years before, the one that accused me of hiding behind books. But if I couldn't hide behind booze, where was I going to hide?

Once we presented our autobiographies, we could get a pass to go outside, as long as we stayed within the perimeters of the rehab property. For Maddie and me, both runners, it was essential that we get our pass and get to running. Some days we ran together, creating a makeshift running route around the parking lot and the large field. We both used running in relation to our drinking. I used it as something I had to do before I drank. Once I ran, I earned the right to drink. For Maddie, running was a punishment. No matter how much or how long she had drunk the night before, she rose and ran six miles the next day. Yet at the Ridge, we used it as a release and a chance to get outside and away. On days when I don't feel like running, I remember the parking lot of the Ridge, and how I had to earn the right to run. It felt much better than running as a way to earn the right to drink.

Like Maddie, I went back to the wine. Not the first night, but I went back, which puts both of us in that 90 percent of people who do. Unlike Maddie, I cannot afford another stint in rehab, and it has nothing to do with finances. It has everything to do with Indie. So I monitor the number of glasses I drink, and call a friend if those glasses start too early or turn into bottles that empty too fast. Though I don't keep in touch with her, Maddie remains a warning I cannot ignore. I sat next to her on the day she read her own autobiography, after days of delaying. She struggled to keep the seventeen handwritten pages of her life in order. Confused and skipping over significant events, she'd search through those pages, as if she didn't recognize her own writing, and apologize repeatedly. It's how I imagine her life, filling gaps with wine and Xanax every time she loses her place.

But oftentimes we can see other people's lives better than we can see our own. After all, Maddie was the one who reminded me on the day she was leaving, as she packed up her oversize Louis Vuitton luggage, that I needed to rewrite my autobiography. "Redo Step One," she said, "but tell the real story this time. Not an essay." For the first time, I took her advice.

19. Point of View

I am in Texas, spending the week with a good friend and thinking how this time last year I was in rehab. In her back yard, barren trees reach for each other against the sky. "It's been a long time since I've been in Texas," I say, even though I'm only talking to myself, feeling where I am more than knowing. "I forgot how the sky feels heavy on days like this. No rain, just the weight of it." Kate says nothing; I'm not even sure she looks up. Kate is the friend I've known the longest. In a picture of us at Kelly Kay's party in 1972, Kate is three, standing behind a table of presents in a yellow dress, picking her nose. Now we are both in our late thirties, catching up on each other's latest stories while her three-year-old son and Indie run around the yard.

Kate's older sister, Denise, is always good for at least one story, and this time it's about how she was able to get on a plane to Mexico without her passport. Somehow she flew across the border without following the rules, a fact that cannot possibly surprise me after all these years. Even though Kate and I are friends, it's Denise and I who have always resembled each other in character. I laugh at the story, imagine her on some beach with a rum drink, worrying about how, now that she's made it to Mexico without a passport, she's going to get back into the United States. Or, knowing her, she hasn't given it a thought. Meanwhile, Kate spends a good part of the day wondering when her sister, now forty, will grow up. I want to tell her that it has nothing to do with being grown up. It's about living outside of the narratives that everyone else follows.

Kate's sister had a daredevil mentality as a child; I can remember her jumping from the roof of their house onto the trampoline; I watched her in awe, too afraid to even jump too high from the trampoline itself. It would be years before I would learn how to take risks and dare the universe to disturb me while I took chances. Things like climbing to roofs and the tops of swing sets were risks I was never willing to take, but Kate and her sister had no problem getting to places that were out of reach to me. In fact, the only time I ever dared a roof was in graduate school, after I charmed a custodian into giving me the roof key, so that a friend and I could get on top of the English building and drink Bud Light until students began arriving on campus the next morning. Even after several beers, it took me a long time, my friend's tireless coaxing, and many deep breaths before I could brave the iron rungs on the wall.

Denise, however, was a phenomenon to behold, and I found myself wanting to earn her attention. One afternoon, when we were all playing at their grandparents' house, she dared us to climb up to the roof of the garage, which was separate from and behind the house. I think there must have been a tree near the roof, or maybe Kate and her sister were both more agile than I, able to scale a wall through careful positioning of feet along windowsills and doorframes.

Somehow I did get up there, but as soon as I got up, I worried about how I would get down. No way could I even access the thrill, or care about being somewhere I shouldn't be. When a voice called us from the back porch, Kate and her sister quickly scrambled down. I put one toe toward the edge of the roof and froze. Eventually, one of them had to confess not only what we had done, but that I was still up there, afraid. I assume a ladder or Kate's tall father guided me down. What stays with me, even now, is being up on that roof, unwilling or unable to move.

When I was eleven and she was twelve, Kate told me: "You're not just an eater. You're a drinker, too." We were at the mall without our parents, eating at Farrell's, our favorite burger/ice cream restaurant, a place where we took turns pretending that it was our birthday so that we could get a free sundae and the drum to boom three times in false celebration. "Some people eat fast, some people drink fast," she informed me, as if there were categories one could belong to in some sort of official capacity. "But you, you're both," she said pointing to my near-empty plate and glass, and back to her side of the table. I had grown up with a father who ate quickly, who moved on to my plate if his were empty, so I learned to keep up with, or ahead of, his pilfering. Where I earned my ability for, or habit of, drinking quickly, I have no idea. Who even thinks about such things? Sure, college drinking buddies and friends at happy hour always commented on my two to their one, but during those nights at the bar, my steady pace drew awe, even sexual interest, from the boys around the table. But at eleven, being a fast drinker didn't hold any bragging rights, especially when it usually meant I was out of root beer. Usually I ended up sucking on my straw while Kate slowly paced sips between bites of her burger. I didn't know what to say; even at that age, Kate's observations rendered me silent.

Kate and I were different. When we went swimming, she wore both ear and nose plugs; I dove from the high diving board. Kate has always suffered from allergies; I write "N/A" on all medical forms. She is a dark-haired, dark-eyed Italian with translucent skin; I am a blue-eyed blond who loves the sun. In high school, Kate spent one year on the JV drill team before opting for French classes and trips to Europe; I became head cheerleader and president of the student council. Kate worked at a clothing store in the mall and saved her money for college textbooks; I worked at a candy store in the same mall and spent my money on wine coolers, which I hid in a compartment in the trunk of my brand-new red Cavalier Z24. Kate drove a used blue Ford Escort and went to college close to home, graduating in five years with both her bachelor's and her master's in accounting. I drove six hours to a college I transferred from after a year, finishing my bachelor's and following with a master's, a doctorate, and another master's after that. Eleven years of school, which meant struggling and being broke while Kate worked, building a retirement plan and savings, buying a house and, after her first child, a Honda Odyssey. Her furniture matches and she has color schemes, like forest green, burgundy, and tan. My furniture is a hodgepodge of thrift store finds and wooden crates as bookshelves. I rent, and most of everything

I own, besides my books, can fit into the back of my Ford Escape, a car aptly named for much of my behavior.

Each restaurant outing with Kate ends with her paying the tab, because, as she says, "You're poor." How can I not be? I've been in graduate school, earning a teaching assistant's salary, while she's made her way up to making eighty grand a year. The last time I checked, my savings balance read $3.86. I imagine the people at Wells Fargo shaking their heads, wondering what kind of woman even bothers maintaining such a ludicrous account. Kate and I both assumed that someday, the waiting pattern I seem to live in would settle into stability, yet the years continue to measure the control of her life against the immediacy of my own. Neither one of us can imagine living the life of the other.

Kate sends large boxes of gifts and clothes to Indie on holidays and her birthday. They are always a week early. Until this year, I thought her son's birthday was in October. It's not.

As a kid, I used to spend the night with Kate at her house on Mark Street, while her older sister slammed doors, missed curfews, and blared Def Leppard from her blue Camaro when she sped us to the mall. Kate was more reserved and quiet, always asking her sister to turn down the music, while I couldn't wait to get my own car, my own *Pyromania* tape. On all those nights she and I spent together, Kate fell asleep early, leaving me eating Pop Tarts and Doritos with her sister, or drinking the liquor we'd steal from the cabinet. When we got older, Kate explained her reserved behavior as a reaction to her sister's, in hopes that she might spare her parents, her mother in particular, hours of closed doors and late-night phone calls. Perhaps. One night, when none of us could have been more than ten years old, we all went to the bathroom together. Kate's sister peed first, followed by me and then Kate, who chastised us both for taking so much toilet paper when all anyone needed was one square. Denise and I laughed, wondering why anyone would even consider rationing toilet paper. "One square! One square!" we teased, as Kate held up a piece in demonstration. Kate is a CPA and a bargain shopper, while I, well, I still spin the roll and grab handfuls.

Kate is one of those people who follows what I call the "narrative of life." College, marriage, house, kids. In that order. I dated Dave, my college boyfriend, for four years before we got engaged, which we did only because it was what we were "supposed to do." Kate was to be my maid of honor, the dresses black, the rehearsal dinner at On the Border. But Dave gave me an out in June, just one month before the wedding. I took it and downed enough margaritas to sleep the shock away. When I woke, I decided I had narrowly escaped the narrative of life, and that I would never read it so closely again.

Kate and I sit on the back porch in comfortable green chairs, where I fill her in on rehab, a story I haven't told many people. It's been a year since The Ridge, and I haven't seen her, a fact that surprises me now, how a year has gone by since such a major event in my life, and how I've never told her anything about it, except for what I was able to tell her on the phone between meetings, when she'd call almost every day I was there. Kate, who has known every phase of my life, is blank here. But this morning I'm too distracted to fill her in. I'm still heavy with last night's dream of Kenny, something I can talk about a little more freely.

"Kenny is an addiction for you, too," she answers. I don't say anything. I figure she's right. But I want to assure her, and myself, that it's not what she thinks. How each dream is essentially the same: "He comes back," I tell her, "and by the end of the dream, I don't want him to stay." I tell her this because I don't want her to think, anyone to even consider, that after almost five years, my dreams are about an inability to get over this man. I turn the idea of addiction over in my mind. Not moving on is one thing, but being addicted to—a man? A memory? A time and place? I'm unsure of how to fill in that blank. Kate says something about my wanting Kenny back. "I don't want that. I want . . . " And I cannot finish. I don't know how. I stare up at the still sky, the craggy branches black against it. I'm somewhere between knowing what I don't want and knowing what I do want. It's where I seem to live.

Kate and I used to make up fart lyrics to Michael Jackson's "Rock with You."

When she visited me after I had Indie, she got up with her every morning so that I could sleep.

During college, Kate and I found something beyond our childhood in common: partying. During holidays and spring breaks, when we were both home, I'd go over to her house to drink before we went clubbing at dark bars, where we used our fake IDs and ordered Sex on the Beach drinks. Kate may be a careful person, but she took advantage of her college days with the fervor of a wild woman. Even after she graduated, happy hours and evenings of wine and *Sex and the City* continued to be staples of our visits. She even picked up her husband-to-be in a bar. Long before they were even married, another friend of ours and I confronted her about the fact that her fiancé had a wandering eye, but she married him anyway.

She told me years later that she considered walking out of the church on the day of the ceremony. Unfortunately, she didn't. She saw all those people coming into the sanctuary and decided it was too late. But how long are we willing to follow a story that renders us small and insignificant characters, allowing someone else to take the main role, no matter how monstrous that role may be? To this day, I do not know what Kate suffered, only that she did so much that she cannot speak of the days she lived with that man, the nights she waited for him to come home. She stayed because she had been taught that marriages last, that her family does not divorce. During those months, she and I spoke on the phone daily, while I worked to convince her that she shouldn't stick to a story just because it's the one she's always heard. She left that man in stages, as most of us do, unwilling to let go of what we know is no good. Just as Kate began to revise her own narrative, her ex-husband ended his own, shooting himself in the heart after falling into a life of drugs and other unspeakable acts. Kate's decision had never seemed more justified.

In November 2006, Kate sent me an email. "I cannot hear your voice," she wrote, "but you sound depressed." Sometimes Kate hears me best when I'm miles away. November has always been a precarious time for my state of mind. When October ends, and November threatens December, I will the end of the year to pass without my knowing. I stopped liking the holidays years ago, when they became an interruption of my routine, rather than a break from it. Having Indie has quelled my annoyance a bit, but now I have my memories of where I was one year ago at this time, when I was actually able to hide away from everything, except Christmas, and it turned out to be one of the most difficult holiday seasons of my life.

For the month I would be away, I told Indie I was teaching at a special school in Salt Lake City, and that she would stay with Jordan, a student of mine who became like a nanny to us during our time there. On Christmas morning Jordan drove Indie the three and a half hours north, while I stood at the front window, watching for the car. If you've never seen or felt the effect of your own addiction, try watching from behind a window as your four-year-old, with a new dress and her shiny black Mary Janes, runs up the sidewalk of a rehab, and see how it feels when she has to leave after two hours and you can't go with her, no matter how much she cries.

But even remembering that, knowing it's December again makes me start missing rehab, the comfort of being around people who had stories similar to mine. I've kept in touch with some of them, the ones who immediately started drinking again, the ones who didn't. Initially, I liked being in that latter category, holding out against odds any gambler would take. After a few months, though, the stakes of sobriety seemed to be too high for most of us; as it would turn out, a suicide, a DUI, a car accident, and psych wards would make last words of some of the notes and signatures in my AA blue book. I felt spared, but barely. I too had taken my first drink in May, when I got a sitter for Indie and drove an hour south to a hotel that had a bar, a Holiday Inn I chose specifically for the purpose of drinking. I checked in, ending five and a half months of clear thinking.

Kate has always been a clear thinker, insisting that logic and common sense afford her the narrative that she expects, so once she recovered from her first marriage, she announced that she would marry again, that she would have a child. Once again, Kate plotted her life, meeting her new husband through Toastmasters, an organization whose members learn how to communicate effectively through delivering presentations and speeches. Though a misreading had thrown her off for a time, she found her way back to fulfilled expectations and no diversions, the way she so desperately needed to live.

One summer when we were in high school, Kate asked me to go to Padre Island with her family. I couldn't go. I had been grounded for the summer, because my parents found out I had been drinking at a party.

While Kate searched for men in promising places, I slept

with married men. As I once told Kate's sister, "When you're in the middle of something, you don't see that it might be wrong to other people, and you don't really care. You're just living your life." And I lived for many years like that, seeking unavailable men or just picking and choosing the men I would sleep with but never stay with. I had no plans, no desire to marry. Even when I got pregnant and Kenny asked me to marry him, I refused, unwilling to give in simultaneously to two things I claimed to never want: marriage and children. I had never envisioned being able to settle down long enough, or be responsible enough, to care for a child. After all, I was the quintessential renter, too restless to stay anywhere for longer than two years. How could I commit to a lifetime? With a man or a child? I could be comfortable being partners, committing to Kenny as each day came, but the thought of declaring my loyalty for a lifetime caused me to shudder. Being pregnant, for me, was too abstract. I couldn't muster the celebration and giddy glowing that I see in so many women. I was just mad that none of my shorts fit after only six weeks.

"But you haven't followed any of the rules" was exactly what Kate said when I told her I was pregnant. Here I was, shacking up in Colorado with a man and an unexpected baby on the way. I could hear Kate asking herself the question without hearing the words: *How can I follow all the rules and not get what I want, while Jill lives minute to minute, man to man?* I'd quote the Rolling Stones here, but it would be trite.

During my pregnancy, Kate got engaged, and so we

joined her bachelorette party with my baby shower. She threw my only shower by flying to Colorado with her sister and some friends, and they all went skiing after giving me a surprise shower in a joint called Tom's Tavern in downtown Boulder, where we took a group photograph in front of the bar. For a while, Kate kept a picture of us from that afternoon in her living room. We are standing on Pearl Street in shadow, the sky hidden behind buildings, she in a black leather jacket and I in a large red sweater, both of us at beginnings, one planned, one not, as usual.

Kate is the only person to ever confront my mother about how she treats me.

Kate once said, getting out of my Jeep, that the only people who drive them are the ones who refuse to grow up.

Kate showed up, unexpectedly, at my grandmother's funeral, even though she had never met her.

Kate tells me that I overreact.

Kate asked me, on a camping trip, to show her how to give a blow job. She had been married for two years, and her husband told her she was trying too hard. Luckily, we had packed a banana or two.

I think of my friend and her life, the steadiness of it, the size of it that seems larger, somehow, than my own. Not because she's had more exotic adventures or gathered more experiences; after all, she has always lived within a sixty-mile radius, while I have lived in multiple cities and several states since high school. She did take me to Puerto Vallarta for earning my doctorate, though while we were there, I watched her parasail and buy trinkets for all of her friends and family members, while I kept checking my bank account at ATMs, in disbelief of my $22.50 balance.

On that trip we were invited, as we have often been, by two men to join them, but when the conversation shifted to meeting up later and smoking pot, Kate withdrew from the fun and insisted we go back to our hotel. "Oh, come on!" I pleaded, as she seemed to march down the beach in front of me, but Kate was firm in her resolve to not be abducted, especially along the beach of a Mexican resort city. For whatever reason, I never allow my mind such possibilities of danger. Kate lets me know when I've gone too far, and in her mind, I always have—even when I feel like I'm just getting started.

Another time, she had a conference in Las Vegas, which was only a quick drive from southern Utah, so she asked me to meet her there and stay in her room at the Venetian, a simulacrum of Venice, complete with streets of water, gondola rides, and a painted ceiling that shifts colors with the hours of the day. While there, Kate and I found a little wine bar along the "street" and spent the best part of our time together sipping wine (still my two to her one). The next day, while she attended meetings, I found my way back to that bar and spent the day drinking and talking to the bartender and other strangers who popped in for a glass or two. I hated to leave the Venetian and the two days that allowed me to pretend I could easily have a life of hotel bathrooms that looked nothing like the stark white ones in Motel 6. In some ways, Kate does have a bigger life, with more opportunities and experiences, though they're just different kinds from mine. After all, I'm pretty sure she's never run through the sprinklers in a city park naked and drunk in the middle of the night, only to be pulled over and thanked by the cop for the view. I haven't told Kate half of what I've done. Or what I do.

Though Kate used to stock her refrigerator with Bud Light before my visits, and though we have been drinking together since high school—even sharing a minor-in-possession charge from a New Year's Eve when we drove to a town our parents had no idea we were in—Kate, I know, has hidden her wine. Since she graduated from college, she has had a wine rack I covet, one that can hold about twenty bottles, and it usually does. I respect her attempt at not tempting me, but how can I tell a friend who has no addictive, obsessive tendencies, my one square friend, that I am my own worst temptation?

Since that afternoon in her back yard, Kate and I have not spoken of anything important, probably because she senses that I am unwilling to discuss it. After all, she has the answers, just not the ones I want to hear. When she drove me to the airport, she asked when I might get back to Texas, probably because I had stayed away so long, almost two years, before this last time. I answered, as I always do, with something vague and noncommittal, always aware that in her mind, I'm destined to float in some kind of alternate universe, a world without the gravity of responsibility and stability, where I drink too fast and get myself into places I cannot come down from.

Two nights earlier, we had been in her living room,

where she told me that I had been a mess for five years, since Kenny, and that it was time to get my shit together. I was surprised at the words, not because I disagreed with them, but because she had never been more brazen in her assessment of my life. And I wondered about the fairness of her consistent comments on my choices while I've never indicated, not once, how I feel about hers. I suppose the traditional narrative is allowed to run free without criticism, but the unconventional one, that's the one everyone feels compelled to edit.

On some days, it's too much, and I grow tired of living the life of some experimental narrative while Kate seems to follow a paragraphed form. Still, I would not want to live such a patterned existence, one that follows without asking questions or wondering about "what ifs." Does she, in any way, wish for part of my freedom? Does she ever long to go back to the edges she used to dance along in college? To know what it might be like to surrender stability for abandon? I'm sure that now and again her past shifts beneath her, but it never seems to unsettle her the way mine does, leaving me unstable.

We hugged at the curb, and she told me to call her if I needed her. I checked my bags, and as I stepped into the doors to the escalator, I waved goodbye one last time, even though she was already driving away.

Significance

20. Driving I-15

I do not want to take back any of the streets I have lost. I do not want to reclaim any cities. I lost Washington Street to Hal. A whole town to Shaw. The blue house on Stover Street to Kenny, though maybe I still have the way the morning sun warmed the kitchen. I surrendered Tech Terrace Park to Jason, along with a bar on 19th Street. Brian owns the second story of that stained glass–windowed restaurant where we shared a salad and too much wine the night before I left town, the night I drove away in my black Jeep, my hand tossed up in a final thank-you at the corner of University. For years I let Mike have the Vegas Strip, though enough years and enough return visits have now rendered it a long avenue of magic, for when Indie sticks her head out the back window in wonderment on a desert night, I need no part of what I should have let go of long ago.

I have always let men have cities, streets; and I shouldn't, because they abandoned them long before I did, leaving me to drive through a conversation we once had across from campus, past the porch where we once read Raymond Carver to one another, by an apartment where I used to spend the night, shower. It's been seven years, and I'm still not going back to Lubbock, Texas, because I know I'd be going back to Friday afternoons in the Sheraton, a balcony on

14th Street, and a running trail, and I'd worry that Room 236 or the white wooden railing or Mile Two wouldn't remember me, as if I had never really been there, was just the shadow that had once followed someone I loved. I tried going back to a house across from the Eagle River once, but the shudders of a summer were stronger than my resolve to say goodbye to it, and I turned my car around before I could even see the street where I had once waited for Kenny to come home, when he was still coming home.

In the summer of 2003, I started west on the way to my new state, my new home. Turned off my cell phone and the Allman Brothers CD so that I could listen to my own stories: the first time I watched my dad lose a football game; the night I looked downstairs to find my brother opening a bottle of wine hours after everyone else had stopped drinking; the way my mother pronounced "I love you" as she left her mother sitting in a yellow chair, because she had never given herself permission to walk away without saying the words; the twenty-six hours Kenny drove that winter after he called and heard *too long alone, too long drinking* in my voice. I kept the cruise at eighty-two and made the winding curves west, talking to a road. I admitted all the streets and towns and corners I surrendered, an avowal that leaves me without a country. I drew a map of myself and of that stretch of highway, so that it will never be his, never ours, but mine.

21. ¡Viva Terlingua!

That year, I was drinking gin and tonics, lots of limes, maybe four, five, at a time. I was drinking anything I could put a lime into: a beer bottle, a margarita, a man's mouth. This particular afternoon, I had wandered into the RV of a gray-haired man named Erlan, and was sitting on a scratchy bench of a tired yellow color while Erlan's shaky, bulbous fingers cut limes on the makeshift counter and he spit out gin shouts into the cramped space of just the two of us. No one I knew was anywhere I could see.

Erlan had been coming to Terlingua since 1978, and he had the pictures to prove it. Longer, darker hair, cutoff shorts, small, perfect squares of '70s photographs showing something I was trying to get to—places I'd never been. I usually revel in no one in the world knowing where I am, but this time, I felt the shudder of *shouldn't be here* when Erlan put his tongue in my mouth. I let him roll it around mine for a minute or two longer, and then I jumped up, clearing the door and the narrow steps, to land in the glare of the South Texas sun. I swayed away from his campsite, squinting at the rugged desert of the Trans Pecos. I didn't know then that there really are no such things as borders, just consequences to crossing them.

Terlingua, ten minutes from the Mexican border and Big

Bend. A town described in all the travel books as "haunting." And it is, but not for the reason the guidebooks refer to; it's a ghost town, all right, and somewhere amidst the ocotillo accents of the plateaus and a landscape marked by seductive absence, there's a twenty-five-year-old me with a flannel shirt tied around her waist, a Bud Light can in her hand, another wedged into a back pocket. Always the crumpled pack of Marlboro Lights tucked into the top of my tank. There I am, pulling down a three-day buzz and telling strangers that my boobs get hot when I smoke weed.

I used to hit Highway 385 South once a year on some kind of pilgrimage to see how far out I had to go to lose myself. Back then, I was living in Lubbock, and it was easy enough to get to the southern border of Texas for the weekend—only seven hours away. I made a road tape for each trip; I still have them all. "Terlingua and Beyond 1997," "Borders 1998," "The Road to Terlingua 1999," each an eclectic mix of '70s tunes, by groups like America, the Eagles, and Earth, Wind & Fire, and good old country favorites. All those years, I lived a life that did not take boundaries into consideration, so I needed a wide expanse deserving of my escapades. The desert shrub region of Terlingua has no fences, no stop signs, not even a billboard to remind me of what is down the road. It's a landscape that truly reflects the rituals, the people, of the place. So, with no barriers to compete, I could draw my own lines, like the one between Erlan and me, but I also knew there were still edges out there, like other men, men I wanted to tease, slopes of stomachs I wanted to trace with my tongue, edges of drunkenness I could fall from.

Once a year, Terlingua transforms into some kind of commune, and I'd hear the call just like a train whistle and would want to wander around the desert in flip-flops, with sand in my shorts pockets. Terlingua turns truck drivers, lawyers, graduate students, artists, and bikers into the same kind of people, the kind who just want to take it all in—the sun, the booze, Texas music, each other. Dozing in the afternoon and dancing crazy in the night, offering a beer from the cooler to anyone who'd get within shouting distance, throwing an arm around a stranger's shoulder, laughing. And during those years I needed that, because I was in a mess back at school, where I was finishing up a doctoral degree, sleeping with Wilbert, and figuring I'd better quit at some point—although that point was nowhere in sight, not even after his wife showed up at my back gate one day, looking for his car. I've always been good at living in two worlds—the halls of the English building by day, the bar stools of some joint by night. Separate, but equally me. But those years I came pretty close to losing the distance between the two, hoping that the questions I hadn't answered back home wouldn't transpose themselves onto the walls of the desert mountains.

Something I always liked about Terlingua—there was no distinction there, just a panorama of abandoned territory, dry, forgotten towns with names like Presidio and Marathon, ominous and daunting. At the end of October, an annual chili cookoff would bring folks from all over the United States. I remember driving just outside of town to the flatlands of the desert, which opened up to rows of

RVs, oversize trucks, and trailers crowded against each other, the way the chili-goers would end up at the outdoor country dance on the Friday and Saturday nights of the cookoff. People were serious about their chili, but also about having a good time. Not everyone was there for the chili; most people were there just because it feels good to be with cowboys and crazy women, with locals and Mexicans who didn't make it far beyond the border before they settled there, with off-duty police officers and big-bellied, bearded bikers.

During the day, booths would offer cups of chili and feature some kind of entertainment, like the Miss Terlingua pageant, free tequila shots (as long as you'd suck the lime from your lover's mouth, and since I never went down there with a man, I always had to borrow one), karaoke (complete with costumes), Elvis impersonators, best-legs contests. And if the blare of "Whiskey River (Take My Mind)" from the Willie Nelson lookalike contest booth didn't draw you in, public relations representatives from the various booths would be roaming the grounds, handing out bumper stickers. So by the end of each afternoon, I'd always end up stumbling around with stickers all over my body. One year, I ended up with VIRGINIA IS FOR LOVERS across my ass.

In Terlingua, terms like "political correctness" and "feminism" had no place, and it was refreshing. No one apologized for anything, except for stepping on toes during a two-step or spilling beer on a blanket. Whoops and hollers and big campfires showed up at sundown, and everything escalated to a high pitch of crazy-mad by the middle

of the night. Sometime before the sun came up, everyone would settle down, settle in, though I'd always pass a
lingering die-hard, still strumming a guitar and knocking
back a Bud Light, in the early morning hours on my way to
the port-a-potty. It was as if all of us needed to cram a year's
worth of craziness into three days. And judging by the way
we'd feel on that drive out of town on Sunday morning, it
was good that we were about to give ourselves another year
to recover.

In the midst of such abandon, there's always a rumor.
And in Terlingua, a regular favorite was that the real Willie Nelson was going to make an appearance. Not once did
he ever show while I was there, but part of perpetuating the
whispering was about showing that you knew the place. It
wasn't important whether or not he showed; it was the possibility that anything could happen. And I'd show up year
after year, daring myself to do anything. And every year
there were different consequences and secrets and hiding
in the life I was living—all that, about three hundred miles
north. I'd go to Terlingua to get lost, and I could do that,
because when I'd look out past the roofs of the RVs, I could
see for miles and not find anything I'd recognize. The openness of space in Texas is dangerous and seductive, the way
it dares you. Confined within the secrets of my life, I'd long
for a geography that would free me, and being lost geo-
graphically is a good way to feel free, especially for someone who's been living too long being lost emotionally.

There's the staring-out-a-curtainless-window-at-3:00-AM kind of lost. Parked cars and streetlights, nights when I don't want to sleep, because there's nothing I want to do at all anymore, really, except go back to a time when I had something to look forward to, so I start smoking again just to invent something to wait for. Then there's the good kind of getting lost, when I'm so deep in the middle of nowhere that it makes no difference what I do. That's the type of lost I got to know in Terlingua, where I'd end up trading my T-shirt for a tequila shot, sleeping in the back of a pickup truck with a man who knew little beyond my name and the fact that I didn't have any tattoos. I rarely knew whose truck bed I might crash in—and that was the thing about Terlingua: No one minded.

After one of those nights, when I cheered on a group of naked men as they took turns leaping over a precariously high campfire, I drove into the next town to shower and get something to eat, but got sidetracked by a bar. Two hours later, I was cut off rather abruptly after I stopped sucking on limes and started sucking on the neck of the denim-shirted man next to me. "No more," grumbled the bartender to Denim Shirt, a truck driver who'd ordered himself another round and passed the glass to me when no one was looking. I knew I wasn't going to fuck him, but I liked the look in his eye, liked that he was sure I would. Instead, I slept in a bag on the ground in three layers of clothes, and the next morning, the sun screamed at me over the ridge of the mountains, and my mouth was as dry as the arroyo down the hill. It only rains about ten inches a year in Terlingua, the clouds rare and still. They never come close enough to make shadows.

Just a few steps from my campsite, Erlan popped out of his RV with a cup of coffee, the steam sifting through the morning air, the way heat did on the highway back home, a road I couldn't see from there. I pretended to still be asleep. But Erlan lurked close like a javelina, and maybe because it was the last morning I'd be there, I started thinking about the border, how it was close enough to cross. Mexico. I could climb into my Jeep and disappear. Hell, I'd even take Erlan.

I haven't been that kind of lost in years, because now there are boundaries—like lack of money and a kid—and it's been too long since I've seen a man look at me in a way that lets me know I'm two drinks away from pulling my sweater over my head. I long ago abandoned the landscape of married men, perhaps because my own man roamed off into the territory of another woman, and I now live inside the damage done to the one who waits at the window all night, not wanting to believe what she knows to be true. I'm too lost now to even know what I'd be running from, but lately, instead of staring out the kitchen window, I rummage through the drawer and pull out my map, run my fingers over the word "Terlingua," my mind across the rugged topography of a former self.

One night recently, instead of seeing the desert, I found Kenny's handwriting on the back of the atlas. The word "chandelier." I had no context for the word or why he wrote it down, the way I have no idea where he is. I flipped through the pages, the states, and I saw other scribblings, lines he drew on roads, mileage he calculated, rivers he marked with a red pen. Here was evidence that he had once been around. He had marked up my map, drawn lines across the spaces I wanted to go to, and for the first time I was angry, because his words had kept me from finding my own direction for so long. And then here was this map, with a word whose meaning I could not place. I had been living a life based on layers of meaning—his favorite songs, his hands, the paint-stained jeans I loved, a palimpsest on which everything was read and written. And then a word I could not attach meaning to, and I felt lost again, bad lost. Even more, I wanted to get back to Terlingua, to a time and a place that exist without his imprint.

So I thought about a return to South Texas, to the desert, to the tart taste of a good lime, to the chance that Willie Nelson might walk into the restaurant La Kiva, to flannel shirts that smelled like wood smoke. I thought about the way I used to feel free. Lately, I've been bumping up against borders so much that I don't even notice them anymore, and I can't remember what it's like to lose control. But when Kenny left, I did lose control, and in a way I had never known. I chose him, after all; I had even chosen to have a child with him, and while I had chosen not to marry him, I meant to never leave.

He did leave, and I remember the morning I found him in the thrift store chair in the corner of our living room. He was crying, exhausted, and just home at 7:30 AM from god knows where. We had been moving through the heavy rooms of our apartment like ocean waves, with white foam that spreads out and dissolves, the imprints of retreating water heavy and dark. Losing control of a shared life is one thing, admitting it is another, and doing something about it, like leaving, is so terrifying that most people never even get there. But I watched him pack. I even helped him separate our dishes, gave him some food from the refrigerator and two pillows, followed him down the steps, and watched him climb into his blue truck, duck his head, and pull out of the drive. I imagined his radio set to the '70s country station that he liked, the words of Charley Pride's "Is There Anybody Goin' to San Antone?" the soundtrack to his departure, because it was the last song he taught me to play on the guitar.

It's simple, really. We all live within control and outside of it—in some kind of delicate balance. We make decisions, and we give up desires, and sometimes that's a two-in-one deal. People like Kenny don't have borders, or control, because every decision is a desire and nothing else ever wins. Something about being held accountable, to a woman, to a job, to a town, had no magic for him. Even if he stuck around, he found ways to escape that wouldn't bother anybody who didn't know. But when he wanted out for good, his mind was made up, and he would go in a way that made other people apologize. He lived "Heard It in a Love Song," by the Marshall Tucker Band. I loved the song, too. I still do. I have to honor the need to get goin', to get to someplace else, never mind that I'm with our daughter, that we are the things left behind.

Kenny's the kind of guy who enjoys the freedom of no

boundaries; It's because he's a lost man. And not middle-of-the-night lost or Terlingua lost. He's the kind of lost that never finds a place to stay, a woman to stay for, because he's never really figured out where he's supposed to be—and maybe that's a kind of place in itself. A place with no boundaries, nothing to keep him anywhere, except driving down the road. But I do get angry knowing there will never be a landscape for me without blue trucks.

One thing that has come from all of this is the discovery that while I want to get back to the open spaces of abandon, I don't want to stay there forever; I want to have some boundaries, because I like having Indie around, and I like being her mother, and I like being a professor. But within all of this responsibility, I know that I need to lose control again, the way I once did in Terlingua, so that I can cross this border, a chasm, really, of the last two years of my life. I need to let everything go just so I can let this one thing, this one man, go. I need to get back to the girl who can drink all day and into the night and sleep way into the next morning, who can take her top off and clear campfires in a jumping contest, who can share a sleeping bag with a man, but not her phone number. I need to go back to Terlingua to find her, to see that she's still there. To lose control and get lost, the good way, again. And when I go next October, I'll stop on the way out of town, buy a new map. A bag of limes.

22. Missing Mexico

It had always been a fantasy of Hal's to leave the Wormy Dog and end up in Mexico, so when he stumbled up behind me around midnight and asked if I wanted to go to Matamoros, I said yes. Five hours before, he had picked me up for our first date, and after burgers and beer, we'd walked over to the Dog, where we lasted two hours before heading out for Mexico.

I had met Hal earlier that afternoon. I was reading *The Catcher in the Rye* at the university pool as he performed explosive cannonballs off the high dive. It was 1999, and I was waiting to begin my PhD in film studies at Oklahoma State University. Hal was in his seventh year as an undergraduate. Taking a break from his cannonball contest, he swam over to the side of the pool near my lounge chair and propped his forearms on the edge. He squinted in the sun. I had noticed him there a few days before because he seemed so carefree, a feeling I never really allowed myself, and he looked like Steve Young, with curly dark hair and a smile that took up most of his face. "No one comes to the pool to read," he teased.

"I do," I said, unimpressed and annoyed by the interruption. Holden was in a phone booth, thinking about calling Sally in the middle of the night. I went back to my book. Eventually, Hal charmed me enough to join him and his group of laughing friends in the pool. It wasn't long before he told me it was buck burger night at Eskimo Joe's and asked me to go. I liked the kind of man whose idea of a date was a burger for a buck. Before I knew it, Eskimo Joe's turned into the Dog, and the Dog turned into I-35 South in the middle of the night.

The Wormy Dog Saloon was a bar on the second floor of a building on Washington Street, just across from campus. It served beer only, and at that time I drank only mixed drinks, margaritas or gin and tonics, so I wasn't really interested when the gang shifted the evening from Joe's over to the Dog. Hal assured me that it would be worth it. It was. Rickety wooden steps led up to the thick gray door, and inside, crushed peanut shells littered the wooden floor. The Dog had saddles for bar stools, and on the back wall behind the two pool tables hung a Budweiser clock, yellowed from being trapped in endless hours of smoke. My favorite touch was the fuchsia teddy dangling from the moosehead behind the bar. The Dog played only classic country music and Southern rock: Waylon Jennings, George Jones, the Marshall Tucker Band, Lynyrd Skynyrd. The only exception to the rule was Jimmy Buffett. The Dog was usually a slow bar, especially on rainy afternoons when guys back from hunting trips leaned against their pool cues and shared a pitcher of Budweiser in the back, while Mr. McBeavy, a local who got his name from Hal's roommate, Brooks, wandered through the bar in a yellow slicker, asking to trade a pack of Dorals for a pitcher of beer.

Back then, Wednesday was Ladies' Night, which meant that girls paid five bucks at the door and drank free all night. The guys had to pay $7, but the discrimination mattered little in a bar full of drunken women. I'd trade one empty bottle for another until "Free Bird" came on, the Dog's signature closing-time song. During the time I lived in Stillwater and frequented the Dog, I developed a taste for beer because it was too cheap to pass up. When I'd go anywhere else, I'd often walk away from the bar with a full, cold Bud Light bottle without thinking about it, until the bartender shouted, "Hey, you gotta pay for that!"

When Hal suggested the spontaneous trip to Mexico, he confessed that he didn't have any money. He just wanted to know if I'd be the kind of girl who would take off in the middle of the night. Without thinking, I told him about my new "Don't Mess with Texas" Visa and said not to worry about it. Hal's invitation was the risk I had been craving for years, the opportunity to do something reckless and furtive. After we told Brooks we were going, the news of our adventure quickly spread through the body-to-body crowd, and as I followed Hal out the door, shouts and whoops and the chorus of "Luckenbach, Texas" erupted behind us.

Everyone knew Hal, but no one knew me. To them, I was the new blond girl in town who Hal was dragging off to Mexico in the middle of the night. As Hal and I pulled away from the Dog and toward his apartment, we made a deal: flip-flops, a bathing suit, a couple of T-shirts, and shorts only. We wanted to keep it simple. I dropped him off at his apartment and then sped in my white Nissan the three blocks to mine, where I quickly threw a few things into a bag before driving straight back to Hal's while Eddie Money sang "Two Tickets to Paradise" on the radio. Every time I hear that song, I see my car lights turning into his parking lot and onto his big smile.

So much of what would become our relationship, starting that night, seemed to be about music. When his second-story apartment door was propped open, that meant Buffett or Waylon or David Allan Coe could be heard from the stereo, and that Brooks was probably cooking and singing off-key in a wrinkled white polo, shorts, and gray flip-flops while Hal grudgingly worked on some overdue assignment. Everyone called him "Hale," after the way his mother pronounced his name. I would meet her in time, even visit her after Hal died, but all I knew of her then was from a phone message he let me listen to on our way back from Mexico. I heard a mother's voice warning her oldest son against running off to foreign countries. What were we doing, she wanted to know, getting married? For months, she referred to me only as "Jill the Thrill."

Around six o'clock the next morning, we were still driving. The buzz had worn off, and we were no longer crazed by the moment or the newness of our conversations. We were both silently wondering what we were doing with a stranger in San Antonio, Texas. We needed sleep, but most of all, I needed a cheap place to stay. Hal had offered the impetuous departure, but I was the one with the "Don't Mess with Texas" card, the only one on me that I knew would go through. We pulled into a Motel 6 off the highway, and I put the first of many nights with Hal on my card. We found our room and both fell onto the queen-size bed. We allowed ourselves only a few hours of sleep. Mexico was waiting.

When we woke later that morning, I opened the curtains, squinting at the reality of what we were doing. Gratefully, I spotted a Taco Cabana across the street. Cheap Mexican food and booze. We scurried over, anxious to recapture the fervor of the night before with a morning margarita. We had three each. We were off. James Taylor sang "Fire and Rain."

Hal told me, "You've got to ask Darren about this song. I mean, the story behind it."

"Why don't you tell me?" I asked. Darren was Hal's younger brother, also attending OSU. During the time Hal and I dated, Darren often joined us at the Dog, his smile almost as big as Hal's.

"James Taylor is a Sigma Chi," he told me. Darren was as well. "Get him to tell you," he insisted.

Hours later, as we approached South Padre Island, a gray curtain loomed before us as a storm hovered above the island. We drove against the darkness, even though it felt as if we were approaching the gates of a carnival that had just left town. We both tried to hide our disappointment. We'd come too far for bad weather, but the night before in the Dog, our thoughts had not included clouds and cold winds. When we finally got to the beach, we didn't even bother changing into our swimsuits. The Gulf of Mexico was murky, the wind harsh, the air chilled. We surrendered our sunny beach plans and opted for another bar, the Sunset Grill, a name that reminded me of a Don Henley song. Our bill was much more than I had anticipated, and I wondered if I could even afford this trip. This Hal. But that night, when we crossed the border, all of my fears were overshadowed by the adventure of tequila and shadows, gift-shop sombreros and the giddiness of having run away. As we crossed one of the dark streets of Matamoros, we splashed through deep puddles of leftover rain. The flip-flops I wore were now covered in Mexican muck. I kept them for years—my Mexico flip-flops—until I realized it was probably unhealthy that I was still holding on to them.

Hal and I drank our way through the next two days in Matamoros and made love for the first time in a hotel we stayed at back in Texas. After we had crossed over the border in the late mornings and in the late late nights enough times to quell his fantasy and my penchant for crossing borders, the hours that lay ahead on the highway began to creep into our consciousness. On the way back to Stillwater, Hal woke me up to listen to James Taylor singing "Mexico." I leaned over and whispered, "I love you," into Hal's ear as he propped an elbow on the windowsill with one finger raised against his face, the way he always did when he drove, and smiled. Those words have always come easily to me, and with Hal, they always would. It seemed as if "Mexico" had been poised to be the soundtrack to our journey. Its beginning and its end.

As I often told Hal afterward, we should have left us in Mexico. Once we returned to Stillwater, we never could recapture the intensity or the excitement of that first night, those three days. I guess I thought it could always be like that, and for Hal, life was. But I had graduate school and two classes to teach. I had to leave Mexico in Mexico. There would be no more running off in the middle of night from bars, or margaritas at some cabana in the middle of the afternoon. But for a while, we found Mexico where we could, in my apartment for chicken quesadillas and a few Tecates, or in the Wednesday nights of the Dog.

But Mexico wasn't always easy to recapture. One night, after I had spent two months on a research project on the films of Martin Scorsese and I fell asleep on the couch shortly after dinner, Hal exploded.

"It's Valentine's Day!" he shouted, standing in the living room, his arms thrown up in frustration.

"Hal, please. This paper has just taken it all out of me."

"I'm sick of hearing about this paper! You're always putting school before me!"

I gave Hal a look I'm sure he was familiar with by that point, the one that said, *I take school seriously and you don't*. One of the things Hal had done for me in the past months was get me to loosen up, to have more fun, to wear a Burger King crown and put my book down at the pool now and then. But that night, he took me by surprise, and the only way I knew how to fight back was to embrace my academic side. Now, ten years after that conversation in my living room, I see how much Hal helped me to find balance in my life, to not forget the occasional irresponsibilities alongside all the responsibilities. It was one of the best gifts he gave me.

"You've been neglecting me," he continued, his voice rising. The truth was, I had. I had to. And in his ramblings, and what was quickly shaping up to be an eighth year of college, he could not see that I had committed myself to something that did not always allow for hours at the jukebox and three pitchers of Bud Light. I was living a life toward a future. Hal lived to avoid the future, or completely impede its arrival. That night, as he stormed out of my apartment, his parting shot echoed long after he slammed the door. "I'll be damned if I'll play second fiddle to Martin Scorsese." Indeed.

At first I assumed I had lost him because I couldn't stay awake on Valentine's Day, or that a paper on *Mean Streets* and *Raging Bull* had eroded our love. I was wrong. Even with someone like Hal, it turned out that I was the one who went too far—dancing with strangers in a bar, or standing up on a bar stool on a New Year's Eve. One night he left me at the bar after I'd had too much to drink and danced with other men. It would be something I did with Kenny as well, something he didn't tolerate either. I suppose there's something in me that has to go off on my own, as far as I can, no matter that some man's standing there loving me and wanting to be with me. That night with Hal, when I realized he was gone, I walked back to his apartment and found him in the hammock on the balcony. His abandonment had sobered me up enough to recognize that I was wrong. He told me, and not in a demanding way, "You just can't do that, Jill." Kenny would later react the same way, and in both cases, all that came to mind were my father's warnings about going wild. And in both cases, it served as an excuse to move myself further and further away.

Years later, I emailed Hal after Kenny first told me he wanted to leave for a while. I asked Hal why he ended things between us, searching through the rubble of our relationship in hopes of finding a pattern lurking in my love life. Perhaps Hal could help me turn things around with Kenny before it was too late; after all, in the ten years since Mexico, we had become good friends. He wrote back, "You gave me everything a man could need, Jill." And he added, "But back then, I thought things would stay the way they were then. I couldn't see that things would change." I knew what he meant. In Oklahoma, Hal struggled against his reputation for blowing things off and just being a good-times guy, while I had a degree or two beyond him, along with bouts of beer-inspired behavior. How could he know then that he would eventually become one of the leading sales representatives in a worldwide plastics company? How could he know that he would train consistently, running one marathon after another or competing in triathlons, evidence of a profound commitment I admired? How could he know that the love of our friendship would grow more complex with each year, and that we would type each other through our most private longings? That we would evolve from a drunk, crazed escape into lengthy, pensive exchanges?

He would write of listening to Diana Krall or Norah

Jones. I'd write about wanting. He'd write about the falling leaves of autumn. I'd write to him about white wine. He'd write about red and evenings at home. I'd write about classes at the gym. He'd tell me his latest marathon time. Once he wrote, "When I hear Norah Jones, I think of you. Not the words, necessarily, but the mood." How far we had both come since Mexico. Sadly, we both felt trapped in lives we had never intended to live. He was married, unhappily, and successful, yet searching. I had a broken heart I couldn't imagine an end to. We were both drinking too much and thinking too much that nothing could change.

Not long after I learned of Hal's death, I read Joan Didion's *The Year of Magical Thinking*. It is the third line of her memoir that stays with me: "You sit down to dinner and life as you know it ends." The end to Didion's life as she knew it occurred when her husband suffered a heart attack as they sat down to dinner. The life I knew ended with a phone call from a mutual friend Hal and I had known in Oklahoma. After the usual pleasantries and catching up, I asked him if he kept in touch with anyone from OSU.

"Well," he answered, "that's why I'm calling. Hal died."

I remember not being able to cry, choosing instead to succumb to the truth of life: that it ends.

"What happened?" I asked, wanting to hear facts and ignore feelings.

Apparently, Hal had been on a training ride at a park outside of town. The autopsy, months later, reported an enlarged heart as the cause of death. I couldn't help but feel that I had let Hal down, how he had called me thirteen days before his death, how I hadn't answered, knowing I could call him back. I asked about Hal's mother. I asked if Hal's father had been around, knowing that Hal hadn't spoken to him in about ten years. But at that point, it was about getting the story, which is a futile exercise. I'd never know the whole story, just the one that Hal and I shared. That was strong consolation that afternoon. Yet I knew that at some point, the fact that I could no longer call Hal would hit me. That night in the shower, my sobs were like blunt punches, and I clutched my stomach and cried into the stream of hot water, feeling as if something were being torn from my body, something that had been an indelible part of me. I gave in to the sobs for as long as they'd come, and when I stepped out of the shower, I stepped into a life without Hal.

It took a long time before Hal's mother stopped referring to me as "Thrill." Even so, I liked her. She was feisty and honest and asked questions. Hal worried that I'd feel like a victim of an inquisition, but coming from a family, and especially a mother, who maintained a stifling reticence, Hal's mother was refreshing. She always had a nice, usually Italian, dinner made for us when we'd visit, complete with wine glasses at each place setting. Hal would trade his wine glass for a beer, while I couldn't get over the fact that his mother served wine with dinner. After all, I grew up with teetotalers.

I kept in touch with her for a while after Hal ended things, somehow sensing a connection between us. For years, I had the feeling that she and I would someday be in contact again. When Hal died, I knew why. I wrote to her shortly after I received the phone call. I wanted her to know how much Hal had meant to me and to my life, and how much we had loved each other. Three days later, she called me and told me the letter had saved her life. She demanded that I come visit and bring Indie, which led to another question she asked hopefully: "Is she Hal's?" When I told her no, I could hear the disappointment, the knowledge that nothing of her son remained.

As Indie and I walked through the Tulsa airport, I wondered what I was doing there. Did I have any right, after all those years, to go to Oklahoma for the purpose of visiting Hal's mom? Was I dishonoring Hal's wife's grief by indulging my own? But when I caught a glimpse of Hal's mother, I knew I had done the right thing. She cried without shame, the way we do when grief leaves us unable to hide ourselves. When she hugged me and held on, I let her. I knew she was holding on to a time when she'd put my things into Darren's room and warn, "This isn't Stillwater, Hale." As she drove us away from the airport, I noticed my letter, folded into thirds, near the console and pointed it out. "I keep it with me at all times," she said, telling me how many times she'd read it, and how she'd called Darren over the night she got it so that she could read it to him. How he cried, saying, "That's the Hal I remember."

"That letter gave us both peace," she announced, the way she spoke about everything, as if daring you to disagree.

As we pulled into her drive on Sheridan I saw, for the

first time in ten years, the house where Hal had brought me many times. I put my hand on her arm, letting her know I needed a minute. I realized I was looking at a house where Hal would never be, where he would never not be. I fought my tears, feeling that I had come there to be strong for her, and that the last thing she needed was for me to fall apart. As we got out of the car in the garage, Darren met me at my door. "You're ten years too late, Jill," he said, hugging me. I didn't understand, but assumed Darren had wanted Hal and me to stay together.

I couldn't shake the feeling that I was being given more credit in Hal's life than I should have, given that I hadn't seen the two of them in ten years, and that Hal had a wife who I assumed had been part of the family. But as we sat down to manicotti, Hal's favorite, and the wine glasses (Darren traded his glass for a beer now), the story of the last few years of Hal's life and the significance of my letter became clear.

Even though Hal's mom had intended to honor her eldest son with his favorite dish for the occasion, none of us ate much. We had all been drinking; I had already had two glasses of chardonnay on the plane, and from what I saw while I was there, drinking no longer just meant wine at dinner. Maybe none of us could face the fact that we were all sitting there at that table after all these years just because Hal was dead. After dinner, we all adjourned to the patio, where Hal and I had once drunk warm Rolling Rock because there was nothing else in the house. Hal's mom lit up a cigarette, announcing that she never smoked, but that since Hal's death, she couldn't stop. Darren was smoking, too, something I had never seen. As we all sat around the table drinking, I had the distinct sense that I'd been granted the privilege of entering a nightly, private ritual.

As the sun set and the air cooled off from the stifling, 100-degree midsummer Oklahoma weather, Darren and his mother began to fill me in. They hadn't liked Hal's wife, and since he'd married her, something that Darren had begged Hal not to do the night before the wedding, Hal had all but disappeared, not from their lives, but from being the Hal they remembered. Much of it had to do with his wife's insistence on having things, things that forced Hal to work extra hard. I hadn't known until then how successful and wealthy Hal had become. I was surprised, and admired him more than ever, this man who had clearly built an affluent, impressive lifestyle for himself and his wife and chose not to insert that into our friendship, instead emailing me about falling leaves and his desire to become a writer.

Hal's mother told me how her daughter-in-law had stopped by the house on the night before Hal's funeral, turning the conversation to a purse she wanted, chanting, "See it. Want it. Gotta have it." Hal had apparently refused to buy it for her, and now she rebuked, laughing, "Guess I can have it now." I cringed at the story, at the truth of the woman who had clearly missed the best part of Hal in favor of the material things that I knew Hal never valued. No wonder he had written words of longing, of feeling plagued by meaninglessness.

Hal's wife had prompted his mother to wonder if there

was anyone left who remembered the Hal she knew and loved, who could share with her all that she had lost. Then she received my letter. Out on the back porch that night, she caressed the pages and read me the parts that had meant the most to her:

> Even though Hal and I didn't have the best relationship romance wise, we developed a friendship, one of the best of my life, after I moved back to Texas. That is when he called to tell me about his Dad, and we worked through that together over many phone calls. Years later, when Indie's father left, Hal returned the favor. Even when we weren't struggling in our lives, we kept up with each other. We talked of our current workout schedules, his marathons and triathlons, our new favorite wines, our jobs, but mostly we talked about how we wanted to live our lives. I discovered that Hal was quite a deep and complex thinker and writer, and I so wish I had saved more of his messages. He used to send long messages when I was living in Colorado about his thoughts, his dreams. Here's one I saved from January:
>
> "I've been pining away for a life I'm not living. I sit by day after day wishing life's little adventures were falling around me like autumn's leaves.
> "Well they're not. . . ."
> "I realized last night on yet another late night flight that I'm gonna have to reach up and shake the tree!"
>
> Most of Hal's messages were like this, and while I wondered whether or not to share this with you, I wanted to tell you that his desires, his wantings, have given me comfort. I think that Hal somehow always knew that he wasn't going to live long, and so his unlived life haunted him more immediately than it does the rest of us. I like to

think he's on an island somewhere giving boat tours (one of his many fantasies); I do know that he wanted a simple life and somehow his life got away from him. I think he felt he had to prove himself so much as a businessman that he lost himself along the way.

Hal has been one of my main writing subjects throughout the years, and I thought I'd send you some of the pieces I've written about him, about us. He's read them all. I just thought you might want to see how I saw him—that even writing this letter, I feel I do no justice to him. The piece "The One Who Took Her to Mexico" was the most recent—so I'm sending that one, and I'll send more if you'd like. I sent this one to him on April 26, 2005, with the subject line: "Long Overdue." I remember coming back from a trip of my own and feeling some sense of urgency to send it to him. His response was brief—the way he always was when it came to his emotions. He simply said, "It's pretty accurate. It just makes me miss you more."

During the next four days of our visit, Hal's mother and I spent most of our time on that back porch, smoking and drinking together, talking about Hal and the men we had lost. I told her about Kenny, and she told me about the afternoon Hal's father came home and cried, telling her he was in love with a twenty-five-year-old woman. I admitted to the married men I had been with, how I had felt when Hal called me when his father left, devastated by the very thing I was doing with someone's father. She listened, as she always had, never judging, just offering question after question and the periodic "huh"—which I imagined to signify a combination of shock, wonder, suspicion, and curiosity.

One morning we sat on the back porch in our pajamas, smoking cigarettes in the suffocating heat. She moved a fan outside and asked me to plug it in. When I got to the outlet, I saw that the boom box already plugged in had a James Taylor CD in it.

"Oh my god," I whispered.

"What? *What?*" she called, as if the world had something else in store for her and she couldn't wait any longer to brace herself against it.

"James Taylor."

"You know, for two weeks after Hal died, it was all I could listen to."

I told her of the connection that Hal and I had with James Taylor, about the story of "Fire and Rain," which I had never had the chance to ask Darren about.

"Here, call him. He's at work. Ask him," she said, handing me the portable phone. I wondered if she ever spent any time in the house, or if every day was like this. "I need a drink," she said. "Can you get me a glass of wine? I know it's early . . ."

"Don't worry about what time it is. I'll have a glass with you," I told her as I walked inside, toward the kitchen. I couldn't remember the last time I'd drunk like this, all day and all night, but there was something very comforting in the two of us hiding away, that back porch like a fort, where only people who truly knew and loved Hal were allowed to enter. I grabbed the bottle of chardonnay that she had shown me the night before, one that Hal had bought on his last visit. I hadn't even considered opening it until I saw the James Taylor CD. I called Darren at work, and he told me the story I'd asked Hal to tell me so many years ago, but that he'd insisted I hear from Darren. According to Sigma Chi legend, Taylor's fraternity brothers had decided to surprise him by flying his girlfriend in to see him. The plane crashed upon landing, hence the line from "Fire and Rain": "sweet dreams and flying machines in pieces on the ground." I told Darren how Hal had insisted I hear the story from him all those years ago.

"I don't know why," he said. "It's no big deal." But by the time "Fire and Rain" played on that CD, Hal's mom and I still in our nightgowns, sweating and tipsy in the middle of the afternoon, those lines, "I always thought that I'd see you again," were a big deal. And even though the story turned out to be more legend than anything, I remembered Hal's words: "Get him to tell you." I did, Hal. I did.

During my stay, I wondered about Hal's mom and her drinking, if she would be all right once I left, if she and Darren might drink themselves away on that back porch. But then I thought about the power of grief, and the search for relief, and I imagined that was what it was for her, not a lifestyle. Once again, I saw a woman giving in to the addiction of grief and indulging it as deeply as she could feel it. It made me think of *Out of Africa*, after Meryl Streep has lost everything and she sits on the crates in her empty living room, drinking wine, smoking cigarettes, falling deeper into the reality of all that she has lost. "When I don't think I can stand it any longer, I go one minute more," she says, "and then I know I can handle anything." Such bravery, I think, to confront and surrender to such loss.

I left Hal's mom on a rainy day in Tulsa and flew back

with Indie, who'd intuited that I needed to be alone, that certain conversations were not to be interrupted. She had amused herself with cartoons and the water hose in the back yard. After our visit, Hal's mom and I kept in touch regularly on the phone, drinking and talking and wondering what we were going to do without Hal.

I realized after several months that I had worried about the wrong woman, as my drinking continued to sustain the intensity of those days on the back porch.

On the thirteenth of July, not long back from my visit, I sat on my front porch in Utah and celebrated the life of Hal, who would have been thirty-five that day, with wine and cigarettes, the soundtrack to *Urban Cowboy,* and a phone call to Hal's mom. The next time I would call her would be from rehab. Only now can I see that Hal's death precipitated a depression that I drank my way further into, until there seemed to be nothing to do but drink. All those years of mourning and drinking over Kenny's being gone, and yet Hal had been more a part of my life, more a positive part, anyway, than Kenny could ever have been. When Hal died, I realized what losing a good man is really like.

Not long ago, I was trying to explain the arbitrary nature of signifiers to an American literature class. I wrote "July 13th" on the board and asked if any of them had any specific meaning or significance attached to this day. A couple of students raised their hands and offered brother's birthday, parents' anniversary. I told them that for me, the thirteenth of July had meant one thing for many years: Hal's birthday. I had mentioned him before; he had become his own signifier. Then I told them how Indie's father had left on July 13th, and how the day had become loaded with memories of rushed packing and denials, with Hal's birthday taking on an "it also happens to be" type of definition. Finally, I added, that past May Hal had passed away unexpectedly; and now, instead of July thirteenth being a day with two layers of signifiers, it had become the demarcation of a realization for me: Kenny's never coming back. Hal never can.

The essay I mentioned in my letter to Hal's mother includes a line from *The Catcher in the Rye:* "Certain things they should stay the way they are. You ought to be able to stick them in one of those big glass cases and just leave them alone." After Hal read it, he emailed back with these six words: "In case of emergency, break glass."

I hear James Taylor's "You've Got a Friend" on days when I need to be reminded, but I turn the station every time, not ready to listen to the song in its entirety. And I wonder about Hal's mother, if she still sits on her back porch alone, smoking Virginia Slims and knocking back chardonnay. I wonder whether people, when they see her in a restaurant or at a stoplight, can imagine that she's a woman who keeps her son's ashes on the mantel in the living room. I have not contacted her since Hal's last birthday, deciding to allow her and Darren to continue their private ritual, grateful for the space they opened for me when I was there. I worry that the constant reminder I provide will serve only to make their grief more tangible. But when I think about it, I remember what she said, about how Hal comes to her in dreams and tells her, "I'm all right, Mom. I'm all right." Then I know the truth: He is with her. He always will be.

23. The Streets of Former Desire

So when the desire comes upon us to go street rambling
. . . we are no longer quite ourselves.
                    —VIRGINIA WOOLF, "Street Haunting"

Virginia Woolf escaped the confines of her reality by taking to the winter streets of London at night. For her, an evening walk offered the possibility of an alternate reality. "One could become a washerwoman, a publican, a street singer," she proffers. Yet the most poignant and haunting alternate reality that Woolf came into contact with was that of her past self. Among the strangers on the streets, Woolf encountered a self from six months before, a Virginia leaning over the railings of the Thames. "Am I here, or am I there?" she asks. A tough question, whoever you are.

She reveals, in the last passages of her essay "Street Haunting," that within the few moments of her journey, she had "sought for a ghost." And I wonder: Which is the ghost, the Virginia of January or the Virginia of June? They will never be the same person, she argues, and I know that the Virginia of January could never step back in time and hold the hand of the Virginia of June and say, "Tell me something that will make a difference." For Woolf, the past self is the one that is happier, more sure. And, she claims, if we could attach an "element of uncertainty" to that older person standing where we stand now, we could, for once, enjoy "perfect peace."

Woolf articulates what I have always known, that only the unsettled want to escape; only the dissatisfied look back to the past for answers. But she also raises a truth that I have never faced. If we have to go, she says, it's inevitable that our journey will include a return.

For me, such a return took place over the winter break after Kenny left. He'd left in July, and it had been six months; instead of searching for answers in the present, in the extremes of distance and silence within our apartment, I found myself looking to places I had not been in years, believing that in some moment in my past lay the fulcrum on which my error rested. Thus, I had a desire to go, not to get away, or to escape the darkness and loneliness, but to revisit the places where I had walked before I knew how the heaviness of true loss felt. I wanted to return to the spaces where I had known possibility. More so, once I arrived there, I imagined the force of an alternate reality rescuing me. I wanted to stand in the spot where a younger and less gaping version of myself had once been.

The first place I had to go was Creede, Colorado, where, on one night in 1997, I drove through the valleys of southern Colorado to escape an impending doctoral exam. *How easy it is to escape such trivial matters,* I think now. "To escape is the greatest of pleasures," Woolf writes in her essay. Now I realize that we never completely escape the tough moments of life. Exams can be put out of the mind with a beer and a dance in the street of a town you've never been to, but the man you love and the space you carved out together are harder to erase. I wanted to get in touch with the twenty-something girl who dared to walk into a bar by herself, three states away from her home and anyone who would recognize her. The girl who charmed a twenty-six-year-old raft guide by summer, ski instructor by winter. A scruff of a man whom Kerouac would have called a "rucksack wanderer," he lived in a tent near a creek outside Creede. That night, we ended up closing the bar down and dancing in the middle of the main street, then making out in the back of a pickup truck I had borrowed from a good friend. For several hours, I was simply the girl in the blue truck. Nothing more, nothing less. I'm sure it's not been that simple since.

So that January, I left Indie with some family friends in South Fork, Colorado, drove to Creede, parked my beat-up car, and walked to the middle of the street where I had once thrown my head back to the stars and followed a man who knew little more than my name. Looking back on my visit, I asked too much of that deserted street, even of the girl inside me who needed to dance. I looked through the windows of the bar, the gift and T-shirt shops, and I willed her to return. "For if we could stand there where we stood six months ago," Woolf writes, "should we not be again as we were then—drunk, wild, and free?" (My adjectives, not hers.) In one moment, the reminder that I used to be a "good-times girl" promised much more than the last few months had, for that visit to a late August night allowed me to see that I can be carefree, impulsive, again.

What had been harder for me to believe, however, was

that I would be loved again the way Kenny loved me. This need inspired my next visit, so I walked back to my car and then turned it toward South Fork, twenty miles down the road, where I once skipped rocks in the rain with a man I decided not to leave Kenny for, a choice he never knew that I had to make.

Kenny used to work on the road, and he'd leave me for months in our tiny basement apartment in Fort Collins, Colorado. We had trust, we had expectations of one another that were never intrusive. At no point did either of us ever consider or believe that we'd stray, that we'd want to, that we'd want to hold the hand of another. But you can be blindsided by opportunity, when you least need it or even want it. And there it is—asking you to take it, leaving you with little choice but to be swept away.

So one July weekend, only a month after I had learned I was pregnant, and while Kenny was somewhere across the country, I drove to South Fork to visit a good friend and her parents. During the first few moments that I stood in their living room, a man with a beard and a blue shirt, a friend of the family's who was visiting his own parents, walked in and introduced himself. Later he would tell me that he felt that something beyond a weekend visit had asked him to come. Maybe it had been me. Maybe I needed to know what I would choose if another reality came into view, like a gas station on a long, empty road.

The next morning, as I started out on the mile-long walk from the house to the Rio Grande, I turned when I heard someone call my name. It was the bearded man, asking me if I wanted company. I had not realized until then how much I had hoped I might see him again, and even though I had learned he lived in Fort Collins, too, I knew that once I got home, I could not see him. I was four months pregnant, and when I told him, I sounded like some biblical mystic: "I am with child," I said, probably because I was still unable to grasp the fact that I was going to have a baby. When we got to the rocky bank of the river and it began to rain, we ignored the increasing weight of the drops and searched for smooth, flat stones, just as I spent most of the afternoon ignoring the fact that I was pregnant.

As we skipped rocks into the current, we talked about water, where it goes, if it's different in Colorado than in Texas, and what binds elements across states, across time. When he asked me what my poems said, not what they were about, I turned around and watched him for a long time. Soon we were too soaked to stay outside, so we hid away on the front porch of his summer home. He would later describe our eight-hour conversation as "things you would tell strangers at a bus station." Over the course of those two days, I knew I loved this man, but I kept that to myself.

In between that July and the morning Kenny left me, I thought of that man many times, though I never regretted my decision. Even after Kenny left, I don't regret not leaving, because I told him I never would. I can still see myself on the edge of our bed, Kenny already disappeared into the distance of slumber, while I sat thinking of the blue shirt, the beard, the flowers in the park where we walked that night. What I did regret, many times, was not holding on to the belief that Kenny and I could feel that rush again. I wanted to feel something, to imagine that I could live a different life, and those mental journeys got confused with a long-haired, bearded man who had survived cancer, didn't watch television, and never made love to me because he said it would be easier on him for the rest of his life if he didn't. Both of us, all the while, honoring the space that Kenny and I had carved out.

I remember the night he left, the last thing he said was, "I want you to love your little girl." I was working to really want my child, and it was the first time that I realized how having her would force me to live within certain boundaries I had never respected before. I can also remember the fact that he didn't tell me to love Kenny. Just Indie. Perhaps he knew that any man who would stay far away from the confused, lonely mother of his child might not have the wherewithal to stay, period.

I couldn't get to South Fork fast enough, specifically to that porch. And when I stood on the snow-filled street facing a dark house, its quiet porch, I found nothing. I even walked over to the bank of the Rio Grande, thinking whatever I had felt or been there might be down at the river. Like Woolf, I found only ghosts. No trace of black hair down the middle of a blue shirt, no rain dripping from fingertips or the branches of cold trees, no midafternoon lasagna or reluctance to leave. I dared to face, once again, an alternate reality, though none of my hesitation to live in my present life remained. That torn woman was no longer there. When given the choice between her reality and an alternate one, she had chosen the reality she knew on a daily basis, no matter how fleeting it eventually divulged itself to be. I was glad I had come, though. I had known for some time that I needed to let go of the Jill of that July if I were ever to believe there would be another summer. Winter may be grateful, but it is summer that is giving.

The desire to go *is* a disease, but perhaps its cure, for me, is the return inherent in any departure. Perhaps there are too many alternate realities, haunting us with their proximity. For me, it's a matter of the distance I'm willing to travel, and right now, it's not to the past or too far into the future. I'm holding steady in the now, and it's a good thing. It's been too long since, and perhaps this is the first time, I've been comfortable enough to not wish for that elusive destination called "anywhere but here," and content with my current self. "Or is the true self," Woolf asks, "neither this nor that, neither here nor there, but something so varied and wandering?" Do all of our combined realities fold into one? For I know well the reality of where I've been, where I'll never be, where I'm glad I'm not, and, surprisingly, where I am. I'm a woman who's given herself over to love and failed, and who now stands both beside the self of former summers and alone. Somewhere between the Jill of July and the Jill of January, I am suspended like a season that lingers much too long.

24. The Last Time

From a journal entry dated February 2004:

Maybe I've written this story in other forms, but I'm going back in to the lines to see if I can read them differently. Somewhere, you're riding down roads with no radio, no handle to roll down the window, in that blue truck I bought with my words. I hated the lack that had begun to define the way we lived. Never mind that my car would be repossessed a month later, and I would take the bus or walk or just wait. Everything disappears. I bought your 1978 Chevrolet blue truck on eBay and paid for it with a poetry prize. Poems with you on every page, in the next room, on the couch, my audience to every draft. You urged me to work with words, to cover our living room floor, our bed, with lines spread around me like coupon clippings. You flew to Seattle, took a train to a small city, and called from the train station. How I wished that I could see the passengers shuffling around you as they waited, feel the strained pull of the train away from the station. We both loved the truck, and I once joked: "When you leave me, I want the truck," to no reassurances from you that you would never. Leave. The last time I rode in the truck with you I noticed a coffee mug in the floorboard and wondered when you had bought it, or where you had carried it away from, how long you had been drinking coffee in a silver mug. How I hated no longer knowing such details, the privilege of everyday habits, convenience store stops. For too long, every blue truck, every grill of a Chevrolet, was yours, and I turned my head quickly, looking for my words.

I once said that I would meet the love of my life on a train to Baltimore. I've never even been on a train, and I've never been close to Baltimore. The only time I was ever on a train was when a Vacations By Rail train stopped in Utah last year during one of their $3,000 tours. I grew up a few blocks from railroad tracks, so I spent my childhood falling asleep to the sound of trains passing by. The last time I heard love in your voice, you were standing in a train station three states away. I remember the way the station looked in my mind, and when I remember it, I have to remind myself I was never there.

It is September. Raining. I sit at my desk, the one that used to be beneath the bookshelf in Fort Collins, the one that faced the window overlooking that small creek in Boulder, the one you carried up three flights of stairs to the last place where we lived together. I am looking at words I wrote years ago. It has been too long. Since both, rain and writing. I get up every once in a while, the way I do, to stand at the open window. The release of a cool downpour. One brown leaf falls, and I watch it float and spin, fall. I want to go out and stand in a fall-colored front yard with my arms open wide. The leaves of the trees along the side of the house surrender to yellow. I want to begin again.

I am home today, hiding away from my life, the one you left me. I am thankful, though, on some days like these; I am sad and want to do nothing but watch something like

Falling in Love. Robert De Niro. Meryl Streep. I rented it once for us to watch. I think you fell asleep not long after they bumped into each other in the bookstore. The next day, DeNiro's character tells his friend: "I met a woman on a train," and you know he will look for her at Grand Central when it's time to go home, and every morning when he comes into the city. I want to watch something that will make me cry. Not for you being gone. Not for me being here. I just want to cry. You remember. No reason. So unsettling to you. Living with a woman who loves to cry for nothing. I decide to write instead. Go to the stereo to push play. The stereo with the green lights that made the living room glow on nights when we'd fall asleep on the blue futon after making love to songs we'd play again and again. It took me a long time to get those songs back, to think of them as my own again, though every once in a while I go to my CDs to find a particular song and I find—still, little by little—another thing that you took from me.

Today I listen to the soundtrack from *The Hours,* the film I went to see not long after you left. I went alone, the way I like to do, found a seat near the back. I remember the score in the opening scene brought on my tears. I cried for months after that, listening to the soundtrack over and over in my car, once saying aloud at a red light, "This is my heart." I felt like I was listening to the score of my own life. I even listened to it every time I wrote during those months in that basement in Colorado. That basement a refuge and a sentence. I miss it sometimes, the damp room I decorated with bits of our left-behind life, borrowed furniture, and lights coiled around the stair railing. The washer churning. The dryer humming through all the hours. The phone on the nightstand like a promise. Each time you called a quickening. Maybe. You might be coming back. A gray blanket on the futon where I slept. It was not blue. It was not ours, the one that finally broke after years of our lovemaking and your heavy frame.

When you sleep in a borrowed bed, you never go to bed thinking, *This is my life*. It's all temporary, just as long as you need the bed. You can pull off the sheets, fold up the blanket, and leave that life in a nice pile in the middle of the bed and walk away. You slept there one night. You, too, were borrowed. Asked if I wanted you to make love to me, said I had become thin, that you could feel my spine beneath my skin. It was my grief, reducing me to a shadow of the woman I had once been. My grief, leading the way to the woman I would become.

I spent my months writing that grief underground, hoping one line might change your mind. Though I wrote about others, I was really writing you—like a color woven through each canvas in a painter's collection. Reading over the words, I see myself stripped, bare, begging. I was not asking those words to hide me; their betrayal was only in their failure to reverse a departure. At least that's how I saw them then, but now I see a different purpose. Like a train I never took, a countryside I never saw, a memory I could not place. I could not know then that the words were taking me, and I only know now that I am here. Now that I no longer look for the blue of your truck. But then, it was as if I were walking on the shore between the earth and its ocean. Between. Every image ephemeral, only a reflection in water that might fade or wash away. I wrote that blue into every piece, whether or not it was on the page. A color so dangerously elusive, as if one ripple would undo all the colors, as if all shapes are momentary, evaporations. It's the blue of men who do not stay, like the one my grandmother did not marry.

From a journal entry dated November 2003:

> It had been thirty-two years since he had gotten on a train and waved without saying a word. No word had ever come, from overseas, from down the road. Lucille had waited for a letter, for his stocky frame to show up on her front porch. With the end of each afternoon, she rearranged the colored pencils on her desk in every order imaginable, hoping to alter her perspective of the world, to transfigure it, to reshape its boundaries, its edges. She searched for new configurations of meaning, but still the color of the blue showed up in the same shades every evening, tossing itself through the window like a newspaper discarded by a young boy on his route.

Instead of pencils and paint, I arranged, rearranged, words, and still the blue of your truck in each essay. Such a calm blue, one that would have never found its way onto my grandmother's canvas. One that I haven't seen since a Sunday in July, except on trucks I mistake, for a moment, as yours. But each time I look closer, the blue is not the same.

On your way to pick up the truck I bought you, you called from a train station in Washington. You were almost to Seattle. You wished that I could see the train station, the people, the 1940s of it all. I held the phone tight to my ear, believing it could bring you closer, or me into the station, though I begin that day to realize that you would see many places I would only hear about. Not just train stations, but camping trips in Aspen, dollar movies, gas stations where you stopped. I cannot imagine all I did not know or recognize during those months, but I remember what made up my life: dark nights and early mornings and snow and a busted defroster on my car and the crossing guard I waved to on the way to school. I remember glasses of Big House Red before bed, slow walks across campus, the yellow blanket on the living room floor at the sitter's, the black coat of my friend Charles, all the mornings when the coffee shop was out of my favorite tea. A black skirt I wore on a sunny day. Sitting on lawn chairs on the back porch in December, covered with blankets, smoking in the cold. I was living a life, but all those things were like collected flowers, crisscrossed stems dropped on the ground after someone had walked away in surrender. All that beauty discarded when you would look at me. I felt my limbs falling away, as if I were all fragmentation and disintegration in the face of your indifference.

A few months after you had gone, when I was still fighting and losing you, I sent you a telegraph.

It is October, a month of slowness and Texas roads. These days hold on to themselves like the last leaves on the tree outside our bedroom window. Everyone goes home in October, I once read. Come home.

I had once asked you to send me a telegraph, but you had been ignoring my desire for months, and so I sent you what I wanted. For some reason, it never got to you. Words lost somewhere between the two of us. Not everyone goes home in October.

The other night, while lying in bed, I heard a train whistle. I had not heard one since moving to Utah, and I have often lamented the fact that for the first time in my life, I do not live within listening distance of a train speeding through the night. When I realized it was indeed a train whistle, I wondered how I could have missed, for so long, the railroad tracks so close, the moving trains, the passing by, the leavings. I sat up and listened, not feeling like a woman who had been in a train station only by phone, not feeling like a local taking a tour on a still locomotive. I didn't feel like a woman who had loved only on trains in movies while sitting on her couch on a Tuesday afternoon. Instead, I wondered where I might go.

I do not need a train to wonder where I might go, or even to take me there, because now I know that I can go. And I am. Going. Somewhere. Inside, I'm listening to the rain and putting away a shade of blue that can now exist only in words. Feeling for the first time that you, you are the passenger left at the station.

Conclusion. The Weight of It All

Not long ago, Indie and I lived in a house built in 1935, or, as my friend Ann described in awe, *when Fitzgerald was alive*. A two-story white house, it had a screened-in front porch and hardwood floors, and diagonally faced the street corner. At night I liked to sit out on the porch, watch the moon suspended in the foggy sky. The heat ventilators were some of the more intriguing attributes of the house. Apparently, in 1935, the chutes built between floors allowed the heat to rise from the ground floor to the rooms above. Cast-iron panels on the top (ceiling) and bottom (floor), held together by two springs, enclosed sheet-metal squares. Indie was drawn to them, seeing them as secret passages, hidden compartments. During the hours when I wrote in a second-floor bedroom, she'd remove the grate from the shaft and hide her treasures of fake jewels and beads, or pretend Polly Pocket had discovered an underground lair. One afternoon, while playing, she accidentally stepped into the open grate and fell through the chute. The bottom grate and sheet-metal casing crashed to the living room floor below. Luckily, she caught herself by the forearms, gripping the floor in terror.

By the time I got to her, only seconds later, she was losing her grip, her eyes wide and pleading. On my knees, I grabbed both of her hands and pulled, but I couldn't get her very far.

"I can't hold on!" she cried. I told her in a firm voice that she had to, while telling myself that I could not let her go. I could see past her to the rubble below, the dented sheet metal, shards of wood that had broken free on the floor beneath her dangling legs. For a moment, I thought I might ease her down, so I began lowering her, despite her protesting screams. Then I thought I might just let go and deal with the consequences. What was the worst that would happen? "No! No! Get me out!" Indie called, as if she sensed the potential of my surrender. I wasn't thinking straight, after all. At her height, the fall to the floor would be the equivalent of my dropping four stories. Easing her down or letting her go were not options.

I started pulling again, this time repositioning my grip one hand at a time while simultaneously getting to my feet in hopes of increased leverage. Then I shifted my grip to under her arms, and in that flash of a moment, I had no hold on her at all. I took the chance, though, knowing it was the only way to get her out because her little body was somewhat wedged into that opening. When I freed her, we held on to each other, both crying. "I would never let you go," I said, over and over, trying to soothe her. For the rest of that day, Indie stayed on the couch, stunned and scared, as if moving might cause the world to fall out from under her again. As for me, my hands shook for hours at the thought of what might have happened if I hadn't been able to pull her up, how I had missed the danger lurking beneath her play. That night, as I was putting her to bed, she told me, "I thought the house was caving in."

After I left rehab, I had the resolve to keep away from wine, but I couldn't fathom not drinking for the rest of my life. I'm sure that's why "one day at a time" is the mantra for all addicts, but even so, I knew the mind manipulation in that approach, recognized one day at a time as a series of days that would eventually add up to the rest of my life. Given my commitment issues, I feared the worst. The first night I drank again, five months after leaving rehab, I went all the way, drinking one glass of pinot grigio after another. Alcoholics drink to get drunk, not just to unwind or to enhance the flavor of an alfredo sauce. That's why they always told us in AA to stay away from that first drink, because it's like a weight that pulls you down as far as it can.

I've come to know that all of my addictions are like that, tremendous weights that have their own centers of gravity, leaving me orbiting in a constant state of involuntary attraction. Yet, unlike the planets to the sun or the moon to the earth, I do have the ability to pull back from that force and free myself. There was a time when married men were the only ones I wanted, though many of my friends suspected it had more to do with choosing relationships with no chance of longevity, much like the ones with blue-collar men. Steel-toe boots and tool belts still hold a seductive allure for me, though I refrain from indulging, except for clandestine glances during convenience store visits or exchanged smiles across a room. Yet two of the most significant addictions of my life, the one to Kenny and the one to wine, have finally separated themselves from each other, and after too many years, I've released the weight of Kenny from the sky of my heart.

I see my drinking like my grip on Indie that day as she dangled in the air. I can keep a firm hold on it, moderating my consumption and drinking only a glass or two at night, or I can ease it down, allowing the weight of it to increase until it becomes too heavy and I just let go, not considering the damage caused by the fall. For now, I'm like the farthest planet from the sun, because I know what the debris looks like at the bottom, how much damage I can do when I surrender to the weight of wine. I'm going to keep holding on. I promised Indie that I would.

Acknowledgments

The author wishes to thank Charles Blackstone, and he knows why. Special thanks to Peter Michelson for asking me two questions that keep me writing. Much appreciation and admiration for Brooke Warner, an impressive editor who opened all the closed doors of these chapters. And a sincere thanks to everyone from The Ridge, especially the men who ride trains in the middle of the night.

About the Author

Jill Talbot received an MA in creative writing from the University of Colorado at Boulder, where she was the recipient of the 2002 Jovanovich Prize in poetry (judged by Quincy Troupe) and the 2003 Jovanovich Manuscript Prize. She has a PhD in American literature from Texas Tech University. Her work has been published in *Under the Sun,* the *Cimarron Review, Blue Mesa Review,* the *Notre Dame Review,* and *It's All Good* (Manic D Press). She is coeditor of *The Art of Friction: Where (Non) Fictions Come Together* with novelist Charles Blackstone (The University of Texas Press, forthcoming 2008). She lives in Stillwater, Oklahoma, where she teaches at Oklahoma State University.

PHOTO © MJT

Credits

"My Grandmother's Flowers" originally appeared in the *Cimarron Review* 148.

"My Two Countries" originally appeared in *Under the Sun* 10, 2005.

"Driving I-15" originally appeared in *Ecotone* 3.1, Winter 2006.

"¡Viva Terlingua!" originally appeared in *REAL: Regarding Arts and Letters* 29, 2004.